Careers in Focus

COACHES AND FITNESS PROFESSIONALS

SECOND EDITION

Ferguson
An imprint of Infobase Publishing

Careers in Focus: Coaches and Fitness Professionals, Second Edition

Copyright © 2008 by Infobase Publishing

Ferguson
An imprint of Infobase Publishing
132 West 31st Street
New York NY 10001

Library of Congress Cataloging-in-Publication Data

Careers in focus : coaches and fitness professionals. — 2nd ed.
   p. cm.
 Includes bibliographical references and index.
 ISBN-13: 978-0-8160-7284-2 (alk. paper)
 ISBN-10: 0-8160-7284-1 (alk. paper)
  1. Coaching (Athletics)—Vocational guidance—Juvenile literature. 2. Physical education and training—Vocational guidance—Juvenile literature. 3. Sports—Vocational guidance—Juvenile literature. I. Ferguson Publishing. II. Title: Coaches and fitness professionals.
 GV711.C33 2008
 796.07'7—dc22
                                    2008001765

Text design by David Strelecky
Cover design by Salvatore Luongo
Text and cover printed by Yurchak Printing, Landisville, PA
Date printed: November, 2011

Printed in the United States of America

This book is printed on acid-free paper.

Table of Contents

Introduction

In today's fast-paced, computer-driven world, physical fitness is sometimes taken for granted, or worse, completely neglected. We have become more sedentary than our ancestors: For example, we drive to the supermarket or even McDonald's for dinner instead of hunting it down or growing our food in the wild. While we don't necessarily need (or want) to go back to our cave-dwelling roots, we do need to balance our society's tendency towards huge portions and fatty foods with exercise. To battle the "super-size-it" bulge and improve our physical endurance and health, we need to stay active.

The thousands of professionals in the sports and fitness industry help us do just that. Whether they are coaching a team of baseball players, leading an aerobics class, or encouraging young students in physical education class, coaches, sports trainers, and other fitness professionals make us fitter and more knowledgeable about the importance of exercise and diet in our daily lives. Rapid sales of weight-loss books and DVDs attest to our need for motivational help. The increased demand for physical trainers and group fitness instructors indicates our interest in getting fit and staying healthy. Increased attendance at sporting events shows our continued desire for athletic competition. Indeed, the sports and fitness industry shows no sign of decline and should continue to employ thousands of athletes, coaches, writers, instructors, and therapists in the coming years.

Each article in *Careers in Focus: Coaches and Fitness Professionals* discusses a particular sport or fitness occupation in detail. Some of the articles appear in Ferguson's *Encyclopedia of Careers and Vocational Guidance,* but have been updated and revised with the latest information from the U.S. Department of Labor, professional organizations, and other sources. In addition, the following new articles have been written specifically for this book: College Sports Coaches, Professional Sports Coaches, Exercise Physiologists and Strength and Conditioning Coaches.

The following paragraphs detail the sections and features that appear in the book.

The **Quick Facts** section provides a brief summary of the career including recommended school subjects, personal skills, work environment, minimum educational requirements, salary ranges, certification or licensing requirements, and employment outlook. This section also provides acronyms and identification numbers for the following government classification indexes: the *Dictionary of Occupational Titles* (DOT), the *Guide for Occupational Exploration* (GOE), the National Occupational Classification (NOC) Index, and the Occupational Information Network (O*NET)-Standard Occupational Classification System (SOC) index. The DOT, GOE, and O*NET-SOC indexes have been created by the U.S. government; the NOC index is Canada's career classification system. Readers can use the identification numbers listed in the Quick Facts section to access further information about a career. Print editions of the DOT (*Dictionary of Occupational Titles*. Indianapolis, Ind.: JIST Works, 1991) and GOE (*Guide for Occupational Exploration*. Indianapolis, Ind.: JIST Works, 2001) are available at libraries. Electronic versions of the NOC (http://www23.hrdc-drhc.gc.ca) and O*NET-SOC (http://online.onetcenter.org) are available on the Internet. When no DOT, GOE, NOC, or O*NET-SOC numbers are present, this means that the U.S. Department of Labor or Human Resources Development Canada have not created a numerical designation for this career. In this instance, you will see the acronym "N/A," or not available.

The **Overview** section is a brief introductory description of the duties and responsibilities involved in this career. Oftentimes, a career may have a variety of job titles. When this is the case, alternative career titles are presented. Employment statistics are also provided, when available. The **History** section describes the history of the particular job as it relates to the overall development of its industry or field. **The Job** describes the primary and secondary duties of the job. **Requirements** discusses high school and postsecondary education and training requirements, any certification or licensing that is necessary, and other personal requirements for success in the job. **Exploring** offers suggestions on how to gain experience in or knowledge of the particular job before making a firm educational and financial commitment. The focus is on what can be done while still in high school (or in the early years of college) to gain a better understanding of the job. The **Employers** section gives an overview of typical places of employment for the job. **Starting Out** discusses the best ways to land that first job, be it through the college career services office, newspaper ads, Internet employment sites, or personal contact. The **Advancement** section describes what kind of career path to expect from the job and how to get there. **Earnings** lists salary ranges and describes the typical fringe benefits. The **Work Environment** section describes the typical surroundings and conditions of employment—whether indoors or outdoors, noisy or quiet, social or independent. Also discussed are typical hours worked, any seasonal fluctuations, and the stresses and strains of the job. The **Outlook** section summarizes the job in terms of the general economy and industry projections. For the most part, Outlook information is obtained from the U.S. Bureau of Labor Statistics and is supplemented by information gathered from professional associations. Job growth terms follow those used in the *Occupational Outlook Handbook*. Growth described as "much faster than the average" means an increase of 27 percent or more. Growth described as "faster than the average" means an increase of 18 to 26 percent. Growth described as "about as fast as the average" means an increase of 9 to 17 percent. Growth described as "more slowly than the average" means an increase of 0 to 8 percent. "Decline" means a decrease by any amount. Each article ends with **For More Information,** which lists organizations that provide information on training, education, internships, scholarships, and job placement.

Careers in Focus: Coaches and Fitness Professionals also includes photographs, informative sidebars, and interviews with professionals in the field.

Aerobics Instructors

OVERVIEW

Aerobics instructors choreograph and teach aerobics classes of varying types. Classes are geared toward people with general good health as well as to specialized populations, including the elderly and those with specific health problems that affect their ability to exercise. Many people enjoy participating in the lively exercise routines set to music.

There are approximately 205,000 fitness workers employed in the United States.

HISTORY

Aerobics has become widely respected by health professionals since it first became popular in the late 1970s and early 1980s, mainly because the importance of aerobic activity is now universally recognized. In addition, aerobics itself has diversified to include many options and levels of difficulty. Although the element of dance is still evident in some aerobic moves, it has been de-emphasized in many classes, primarily to encourage those who are less coordinated to participate. Instead of focusing on coordinated dance steps or complicated routines that are difficult to memorize, aerobic workouts now are more focused on a series of movements that aim to elevate the heart rate and work various muscle groups. For example, a particular class may seek to shape and tone specific muscle groups, such as the abdominals or hamstrings. This past decade has seen the introduction of several new branches of aerobics, including water aerobics, step aerobics, interval training, and interval circuit training.

Water aerobics is a popular form of low-impact aerobics. Impact refers to the stress placed on joints and bones during exercise. Because the water supports the body and creates resistance, it is an ideal exercise medium. Provided participants wear the proper safety equipment and are in the presence of others, they don't necessarily need to know how to swim, because in most classes, all the movements are done standing upright or holding onto the side of the pool. Water aerobics is especially well suited to older individuals because the water can be therapeutic for aching joints and muscles.

Another popular fitness class is step aerobics. In 1986, an aerobics instructor and body builder named Gin Miller developed a formal step training program after using the technique to recover from a knee injury. Basically, step aerobics involves the use of a specially designed stool or bench that sits from four to 12 inches off the ground. Participants step up and down in different patterns, which provides an excellent cardiovascular workout.

Another exercise trend is called interval training. In the late 1980s, Arlette Perry, an exercise physiologist with the University of Miami's Human Performance Laboratory, determined that alternating intense exercise movements with slower-paced movements was better for aerobic fitness than a steady level of exercise, because it achieves higher heart rates. Interval classes today incorporate many different types of exercise to raise and maintain participants' heart rates, for example, blending high-impact aerobic moves with lower intensity exercises, such as marching in place or stretching.

Today, aerobics classes are often used in cross training, where amateur and professional athletes combine several different fitness activities to train for a certain sport. A popular workout is circuit training or interval circuit training, which combines aerobic exercise with weight lifting for a full body workout. In circuit training, the workout equipment is arranged to work one group of muscles at a time, alternating so that one set of muscles can rest while the next group is worked. As the athlete moves through each piece of equipment in the circuit, the heart rate remains elevated, without the participants tiring as quickly as they would if repeating the same exercise.

THE JOB

Three general levels of aerobics classes are recognized today: low impact, moderate, and high intensity. A typical class starts with warm-up exercises (slow stretching movements to loosen up muscles), followed by 35 to 40 minutes of nonstop activity to raise the heart rate, then ends with a cool-down period of stretching and

An aerobics instructor leads a class. *(John Birdsall, The Image Works)*

slower movements. Instructors teach class members to monitor their heart rates and listen to their bodies for signs of personal progress.

Aerobics instructors prepare activities prior to their classes. They choose exercises to work different muscles and accompany these movements to music during each phase of the program. Generally, instructors use upbeat music for the more intense exercise portion and more soothing music for the cool-down period. Instructors demonstrate each step of a sequence until the class can follow along. Additional sequences are added continuously as the class progresses, making up a longer routine that is set to music. Most classes are structured so that new participants can start any given class. The instructor either faces the rest of the room or faces a mirror in order to observe class progress and ensure that participants do exercises correctly. Many aerobics instructors also lead toning and shaping classes. In these classes, the emphasis is not on aerobic activity but on working particular areas of the body. An instructor begins the class with a brief aerobic period followed by stretching and weight-bearing exercises that loosen and work major muscle groups.

REQUIREMENTS

High School

Aerobics instructors should hold a high school diploma. If you are interested in a fitness career, take courses in physical education, biology, and anatomy. In addition, be involved in sports, weight lifting, or dance activities to stay fit and learn to appreciate the value of exercise.

Postsecondary Training

Although it isn't always necessary, a college degree will make you more marketable in the fitness field. Typically, aerobics instructors do not need a college education to qualify for jobs; however, some employers may be more interested in candidates with a balance of ability and education.

Certification or Licensing

Most serious aerobics instructors become certified. Certification is not required in most states, but most clients and fitness companies expect these professionals to have credentials to prove their worth.

Certifying agencies include the following: Aerobics and Fitness Association of America, IDEA Health and Fitness Association, American Fitness Professionals and Associates, American College of Sports Medicine, American Council on Exercise, and National Academy of Sports Medicine. Aerobics instructors should also be certified in cardiopulmonary resuscitation (CPR) before finding a job.

In addition, aerobics instructors are expected to keep up to date with their fields by becoming thoroughly familiar with the latest knowledge and safety practices. They must take continuing education courses and participate in seminars to keep their certification current.

Other Requirements

Aerobics instructors are expected to be physically fit, but are not expected to be specimens of human perfection. For example, members of an aerobics class geared to overweight people might feel more comfortable with a heavier instructor; a class geared towards the elderly may benefit from an older instructor.

EXPLORING

A visit to a health club, park district, or YMCA aerobics class is a good way to observe the work of aerobics instructors. Part-time or summer jobs are sometimes available for high school students in these facilities. It may also be possible to volunteer in a senior citizen center where aerobics classes are offered.

If possible, enroll in an aerobics class to experience firsthand what their jobs entail and to see what makes a good instructor.

Aerobics instructor workshops are taught to help prospective instructors gain experience. These are usually offered in adult education courses at such places as the YMCA. Unpaid apprenticeships are also a good way for future instructors to obtain supervised experience before teaching classes on their own. The facility may allow prospective aerobics instructors to take their training class for free if there is a possibility that they will work there in the future.

EMPLOYERS

Most aerobics instructors work for fitness centers and gymnasiums. Most employers are for-profit businesses, but some are community-based, such as the YMCA or a family center. Other job possibilities can be found in corporate fitness centers, colleges, retirement centers, and resorts.

Most medium to large cities have one or more gyms or fitness centers; however, smaller towns may not have any such facilities. There may be limited openings at retirement homes, schools, and community centers in these small towns.

STARTING OUT

Students should use their schools' career services offices for information on available jobs. Often, facilities that provide training or internships will hire or provide job leads to individuals who have completed programs. Students can also find jobs through classified ads and by applying to health and fitness clubs, YMCAs, YWCAs, Jewish community centers, local schools, park districts, church groups, and other fitness organizations. Because exercise is understood to be a preventive measure for many health and medical problems, insurance companies often reward businesses that offer fitness facilities to their employees with lower insurance rates. As a result, students should consider nearby companies for prospective aerobics instructor positions.

ADVANCEMENT

Experienced aerobics instructors can become instructor trainers, providing tips and insight on how to lead a class and what routines work well.

A bachelor's degree in either sports physiology or exercise physiology is especially beneficial for those who want to advance to the position of health club director or to teach corporate wellness programs.

EARNINGS

Aerobics instructors are usually paid by the class and generally start out at about $10 per class. Experienced aerobics instructors can earn up to $50 or $60 per class. The U.S. Department of Labor reports that fitness workers such as aerobics instructors had median annual earnings of $25,910 in 2006. The lowest paid 10 percent earned less than $14,880, and the highest paid 10 percent earned more than $56,750 per year.

A compensation survey by health and fitness organization IDEA reports that many employers offer health insurance and paid sick and vacation time to full-time employees. They also may provide discounts on products sold in the club (such as shoes, clothes, and equipment) and free memberships to use the facility.

WORK ENVIRONMENT

Most aerobics classes are held indoors. Depending on the popularity of the class and/or instructor, aerobics classes can get crowded and hectic at times. Instructors need to keep a level head and keep a positive, outgoing personality in order to motivate people and keep them together. It is important that aerobics instructors make the class enjoyable yet challenging so that members will return class after class. They also need to be unaffected by complaints of class members, some of whom may find the routines too hard, too easy, or who may not like the music selections. Instructors need to realize that these complaints are not personal attacks.

OUTLOOK

Because of the country's ever-expanding interest in health and fitness, the U.S. Department of Labor predicts that the job outlook for aerobics instructors should remain strong through 2014, with much faster than average growth. As the population ages, more opportunities will arise to work with the elderly in retirement homes. Large companies and corporations are also interested in keeping insurance costs down by hiring aerobics instructors to hold classes for their employees. The struggle with obesity in the United States will also have an effect on the popularity and demand for aerobics instructors. As communities, schools, and individuals attempt to shed the pounds, the need for fitness instructors and motivators will continue.

FOR MORE INFORMATION

For information on certification, contact
Aerobics and Fitness Association of America
15250 Ventura Boulevard, Suite 200
Sherman Oaks, CA 91403-3215

Tel: 877-968-7263
Email: contactAFAA@afaa.com
http://www.afaa.com

For information on certification, contact
American College of Sports Medicine
PO Box 1440
Indianapolis, IN 46206-1440
Tel: 317-637-9200
http://www.acsm.org

For more information about certification and careers in fitness,
contact the ACE.
American Council on Exercise (ACE)
4851 Paramount Drive
San Diego, CA 92123-1449
Tel: 800-825-3636
Email: support@acefitness.org
http://www.acefitness.org

For information on home study and various fitness certifications,
contact
American Fitness Professionals and Associates
PO Box 214
Ship Bottom, NJ 08008-0234
Tel: 609-978-7583
Email: afpa@afpafitness.com
http://www.afpafitness.com

For fitness facts and articles and information on certification, visit
the IDEA Web site.
IDEA Health and Fitness Association
10455 Pacific Center Court
San Diego, CA 92121-4339
Tel: 800-999-4332
Email: contact@ideafit.com
http://www.ideafit.com

For information on certification, contact
National Academy of Sports Medicine
26632 Agoura Road
Calabasas, CA 91302-1954
Tel: 800-460-NASM
http://www.nasm.org

Athletic Directors

OVERVIEW

Athletic directors coordinate and oversee athletic programs at public and private colleges and universities. They manage staff; calculate budgets; negotiate broadcasting and other business contracts; raise funds to meet budget shortfalls; ensure that their programs meet academic-, financial-, and gender-related compliance issues; and serve as the public faces of their institutions' athletic programs by talking with media and fans. Athletic directors may also be called *directors of athletics, athletic directors of intercollegiate athletics,* and *athletic administrators.*

HISTORY

The National Collegiate Athletic Association (NCAA) was formed in 1905 to address violence in intercollegiate football. Around this time, the position of athletic director was formally created by college administrators who saw the need for experienced professionals to run their institutions' athletic programs.

After World War II, the NCAA began to regulate and monitor recruiting and financial aid issues. With rule changes and NCAA regulation, college athletics blossomed in the second half of the 20th century. Athletic directors played an important role in the growth of collegiate athletics during this time, but it was not until the First and Second National Conferences on Athletic Administration in Colleges and Universities in 1959 and 1962, respectively, that these professionals began to take the first steps toward creating a professional organization.

At the third such conference in 1965, the National Association of Collegiate Directors of Athletics (NACDA) was founded to serve the needs of athletic directors at junior and four-year colleges. The association boasts a membership of more than 6,100 athletic directors and associate and assistant athletic directors at NCAA, National Association of Intercollegiate Athletics (NAIA), and National Junior College Athletic Association (NJCAA) colleges throughout the United States.

In 1979, the Council of Collegiate Women Athletic Administrators was created to enhance opportunities for women in intercollegiate athletics. To better represent its members, the Council was renamed the National Association of Collegiate Women Athletics Administrators (NACWAA) in 1992. The NACWAA has nearly 1,200 members.

THE JOB

Athletic directors plan and implement athletic programs at colleges and universities. Athletic directors at large Division I schools oversee large budgets, supervise staffs that range from dozens to hundreds of employees, and make many important decisions daily. They are helped by assistant and associate athletic directors who specialize in financial, media relations, compliance, and other issues. Athletic directors at large schools spend much of their time raising money and marketing their programs to the public. At small colleges, athletic directors work alone or with very small staffs. In addition to their main duties, they might drive athletes to games, coach sports teams, write press releases or marketing copy, and teach classes. The work of athletic directors can be divided into the following general areas: staff management/administration, financial issues, compliance, and public relations.

Staff management/administration. Athletic directors hire and supervise coaches and other department staff. They evaluate the performance of coaches and give them feedback. Athletic directors may have to fire coaches who fail to perform up to expectations.

Athletic directors have many administrative duties. They oversee coaches, athletic teams, and employees who assist with ticket sales, fund-raising, public relations, and other tasks. They make sure that stadiums, playing fields, and training, locker, and weight rooms are in good condition. Athletic directors meet with athletic directors from other schools and conference and association officials to coordinate athletic schedules and discuss rules and regulations. They meet with faculty representatives regarding academic issues relating to student-athletes.

Financial issues. Athletic directors create and manage the athletic budgets at their institutions. When creating budgets, they make sure that each sport is allotted enough money to operate effectively. Athletic directors must be aware of their institutions' spending rules, as well as the regulations established by the NCAA, the NAIA, and the NJCAA. They plan and oversee ticket sales and certify income reports from these sales. Athletic directors negotiate radio and television broadcasting contracts and other commercial contracts and agreements that earn revenue for their institutions. This revenue is used for scholarships, team equipment, travel expenses, coaching and administrative staff salaries, the design and printing of schedules and marketing materials, and other expenses. Revenue also comes from fans (known as *boosters*), who make donations to the program. Athletic directors must be expert fund-raisers to make up for any budget shortfalls.

Compliance. Navigating compliance issues relating to academic achievement, scholarships, gender issues, and other regulations established by their institutions; athletic conferences; the NCAA, NAIA, and NJCAA; and the federal government is one of the most critical tasks for athletic directors. They monitor the academic and graduation rates of student-athletes, and meet with student-athletes, parents, and faculty to resolve problems. If an athletic director's institution participates in federal student financial aid programs, they must prepare an annual Equity in Athletics Disclosure Act Report to account for scholarships. The director must also ensure that the institution is compliant with Title IX regulations, which guarantee the equal participation of women in collegiate sports.

Public relations. Athletic directors must be highly skilled at public relations. They need to develop strong relationships with donors and booster organizations that help raise much-needed revenue for their departments. They also speak at high schools, fan fests, and sports awards dinners. They oversee staff that produces and disseminates public relations material about the athletic program.

Athletic directors meet with newspaper, radio, and television reporters almost daily. They answer a variety of questions from these media professionals. They might be asked about the job security of the women's basketball coach, a generous gift to the athletic department by a donor, or the construction of the school's new multipurpose sports arena. Athletic directors speak at news conferences, on sports talk shows, and at other media events.

Athletic directors employed at small schools may only work part time. They spend the rest of their time teaching classes, chairing the physical education department, or coaching sports. All athletic directors, whether employed by a tiny sports program or a major, well-known program, must have a vision for the future of their programs. They must be able to explain this vision to administration officials, the media, and fans.

REQUIREMENTS

High School

A well-rounded education is important for anyone interested in becoming an athletic director. In high school, take accounting, mathematics, business, social studies, and other college preparatory classes. Since communication skills are of utmost importance to athletic directors, be sure to take English and speech courses as well.

Postsecondary Training

A bachelor's degree in sports administration, physical education, or a related field is the minimum educational requirement to become an athletic director. You will need a graduate degree to be hired by the best programs.

Ohio University in Athens, Ohio, has the oldest program in the country in sports administration. Administered by the School of Recreation and Sports Sciences within Ohio University's College of Health and Human Services, the program requires 55 credit hours (five of which are completed during an internship) and leads to a master of sports administration degree. The curriculum focuses on business administration, journalism, communications, management, marketing, sports administration, and facility management. The required internship lasts from three months to a year, and internship opportunities are provided by more than 400 different organizations worldwide. The university also offers an undergraduate major in sports management.

Other Requirements

To be successful in this career, you need to have a love and knowledge of sports. Since athletic directors must juggle many different tasks at once, you need to be organized and able to delegate tasks. Developing strong people skills will help you work effectively with people from all types of backgrounds. You must be dedicated to academic excellence and have a high degree of integrity, as well as have strong management and leadership skills. Athletic directors are under constant pressure to create winning, financially sound programs. For this reason, you must be emotionally steady, a good judge of coaching ability, and expert at business and financial management.

EXPLORING

Reading industry publications is a good way to learn more about this career. The NACDA publishes *Athletics Administration,* a bimonthly journal that focuses on issues in collegiate athletics administration.

The journal also has a Q&A Forum, where leading athletic directors are interviewed about current issues in the field. To learn more, visit the NACDA's Web site, http://www.nacda.com. The NACWAA publishes the *NACWAA Newsletter*. Recent issues featured articles on writing top-flight resumes and developing leadership skills. Visit http://www.nacwaa.org to read a sample issue of the newsletter.

If your high school has a large sports program, it might employ an athletic director. If so, talk with this person about his or her career. Good questions to ask include: What are your primary and secondary job duties? What type of training did you receive to qualify for this job? How did you get hired for this position? And how does working as a high school athletic director compare to working at the college level? If your school doesn't employ an athletic director, ask your guidance counselor or physical education teacher to set up an information interview with one at a nearby college.

EMPLOYERS

Nearly every college and university in the United States employs athletic directors. Opportunities exist at private and public institutions, community colleges, and universities both large and small. At a smaller college, a coach, not a traditional administrator, may serve as the athletic director. High schools with large sports programs may also employ athletic directors.

STARTING OUT

Professional publications such as the *Chronicle of Higher Education* (http://www.chronicle.com) and *NCAA News* (http://www.ncaa.org) have job listings for athletic directors. The human resources departments in most colleges and universities maintain listings of job openings at the institution and often advertise the positions nationally. The College and University Professional Association for Human Resources also has job listings at its Web site, http://www.cupahr.org.

Landing a job as an athletic director can be difficult; dozens of applicants may apply for a single position. For this reason, it is very important that you gain experience in the field and develop good networking skills. Work as a coach, assistant athletic director, or physical education instructor, or in another related position to get experience. Take advantage of any networking opportunities (league meetings, trade shows, association membership) to get to know others working in the field. Some of the best job leads in the industry come by word of mouth. The NACDA also offers internships for aspiring athletic administrators.

ADVANCEMENT

Athletic directors advance by taking positions at larger schools or at institutions that have better-known athletic programs. For example, an athletic director at a small Division II school might take a job at a larger, Division I institution. Or a director who is already at the top college level may take a position at a school that has a better-known athletic program. Some athletic directors become administrators in professional sports, commissioners of athletic conferences, or recreation administrators for cities or towns. Others choose to leave the profession entirely, working as deans or academic advisors at their universities.

EARNINGS

Salaries for college administrators vary widely among two-year and four-year colleges and among public and private institutions, but they are generally comparable to those of college faculty. According to the U.S. Department of Labor, in 2006 the median salary for education administrators (which include athletic directors) was $73,990. The lowest paid 10 percent of administrators earned $41,120 or less per year, while the highest paid made $137,900 or more annually.

Most athletics directors receive benefits packages that include health insurance, paid vacation, and sick leave.

WORK ENVIRONMENT

Athletic directors work in a typical business office setting. Athletic directors at large schools have their own offices and large administrative staffs, while directors at small schools may have to share an office and do much of the work associated with this position themselves.

Athletic directors often work more than 40 hours a week, including evenings and weekends. They travel to professional conferences, to league meetings, and to other colleges for important games. They might be on the road an entire weekend for an important football game or a few weekdays for league or association meetings.

OUTLOOK

The U.S. Department of Labor predicts that overall employment for education administrators (which include athletic directors) will grow about as fast as the average for all occupations through 2014. The total number of athletic directors employed by colleges and universities remains fairly steady. Athletic directors also have little job security. They often lose their jobs if their athletic program fails to meet expectations. While many colleges and universities may cut athletic budgets, some new opportunities may become available as others add new programs. Competition for these positions, however, will be stiff.

FOR MORE INFORMATION

For information on internships, educational opportunities, job listings, and the journal Athletics Administration, *contact*
National Association of Collegiate Directors of Athletics
24651 Detroit Road
Westlake, OH 44145-2524
Tel: 440-892-4000
http://www.nacda.com

For information on student membership and the NACWAA *Newsletter, contact*
National Association of Collegiate Women Athletics
    Administrators (NACWAA)
5018 Randall Parkway, Suite 3
Wilmington, NC 28403-2829
Tel: 910-793-8244
http://www.nacwaa.org

For information on degrees in sports administration and sport management, contact
Sports Administration/Facility Management Program
Ohio University
E148 Grover Center
Athens, OH 45701-2979
Tel: 740-593-4666
Email: sportsad@ohiou.edu
http://www.sportsad.ohio.edu

College Sports Coaches

OVERVIEW

College sports coaches teach individuals or members of a team the skills associated with a particular sport. A coach prepares his or her team for competition and gives instruction from a vantage point near the playing area during competition. There are nearly 30,000 college sports coaches employed in the United States.

HISTORY

The first intercollegiate sports contest in the United States was held between Harvard University and Yale University in 1852. Harvard defeated Yale in a crew (rowing) contest that was watched by hundreds, and possibly thousands, of spectators. In 1856, Harvard University, Brown University, Yale University, and Trinity College formed the College Rowing Association.

During the 1860s and 1870s, baseball, football, and track and field became popular intercollegiate sports. According to Andrew Zimbalist's *Unpaid Professionals: Commercialism and Conflict in Big-Time Sports* (Princeton, N.J.: Princeton University Press, 2001), college football games were attracting tens of thousands of fans and earning colleges and universities significant revenues by the 1880s.

The National Collegiate Athletic Association (NCAA) was formed in 1905 to reform intercollegiate football, where the lack of protective equipment and the dangerous flying wedge formation had caused 330 player deaths between 1890 and 1905. After World War II, the NCAA began to regulate and monitor recruiting and financial

QUICK FACTS

School Subjects
Physical education
Speech

Personal Skills
Communication/ideas
Helping/teaching
Leadership/management

Work Environment
Indoors and outdoors
Primarily multiple locations

Minimum Education Level
Some postsecondary training

Salary Range
$13,990 to $44,200 to
  $2,100,000+

Certification or Licensing
None available

Outlook
Faster than the average

DOT
153

GOE
01.10.01

NOC
5252

O*NET-SOC
27-2022.00

aid issues. With rule changes and NCAA regulation, college athletics blossomed in the second half of the 20th century.

Today, college athletics is big business in the United States, and top-performing college sports coaches and players—especially in men's Division I basketball and football programs—earn their universities millions of dollars in broadcasting and marketing revenue.

In addition to such high-profile sports as basketball and football, college coaches teach male and female athletes baseball, cross country, fencing, field hockey, golf, gymnastics, ice hockey, lacrosse, rowing, skiing, soccer, softball, swimming/diving, tennis, track, volleyball, water polo, and wrestling.

THE JOB

Regardless of the sport they coach—whether it is men's Division I-A college basketball, women's softball at a tiny Division III school, or wrestling at a junior college—college sports coaches are teachers. They must be able to teach their athletes the rules, techniques, and strategies for their respective sports. If they are unable to convey this knowledge, their athletes won't be able to improve their performance and win games.

To teach athletes, coaches plan and implement training and practice sessions. During these sessions, they teach players proper rules, stances, and movements of a game. Coaches use lectures and demonstrations to show their players the proper way to compete in the sport. They point out mistakes and deficiencies and help players to improve their overall performance. Coaches oversee practices and workouts to help athletes develop fundamentals and condition their bodies for the rigors of competition.

In addition to physical preparation, college sports coaches must prepare their players mentally for competition. They give pep talks before, during, and after games to help build players' confidence. During a losing streak, a coach might give his or her team a pep talk to encourage team members to remain confident in their abilities, or may speak to an individual player who has lost confidence in his or her play. Conversely, a coach might talk with his or her team during a long winning streak to ensure that the players do not become overconfident. Some college coaches have a very emotional style that often inspires their players to top performance. This style can backfire if a coach becomes too emotional or even confrontational when dealing with his or her players. A good coach realizes that yelling or even berating players for mistakes or poor play tends to create negative results.

College sports coaches also help their players develop good sportsmanship, ethics, and academic excellence. They teach their players how to act on and off the playing field. They might institute a dress code or a code of conduct for their players to encourage discipline and appropriate behavior. Coaches may act as mentors to players who are experiencing personal problems. They also work to ensure that each of their players meets NCAA academic requirements. Players who fail to meet these requirements cannot play until they improve their grades.

To prepare for competition, coaches meet with their assistant coaches to formulate and develop game plans. They explain and demonstrate their game plans to players during practice. For example, a basketball coach may teach his or her players a new defensive strategy that aims to stop the opposing team's top scorer. A baseball coach may educate his or her hitters about a weakness discovered by watching game film of the opposing team's starting pitcher. A golf coach may discuss the challenges of the course for the next match. Coaches also choose a starting lineup and determine substitution patterns for the remaining players. They must make sure that each player knows what his or her role will be during the game.

During competition, coaches discuss strategy with assistant coaches, yell out plays or encouragement to their players, prepare players who are about to enter the game, and call timeouts when necessary. They analyze the play of their team and the opposing team and change game plans if necessary during timeouts or other breaks in action. For example, a college basketball coach may notice that the opposing team's players are tiring and take advantage of this by instructing his or her players to play a more aggressive defense.

Coaches must know the mental and physical abilities of their players and use this knowledge to make split-second decisions during competition. They must know who is their most tenacious defender, who is their best scorer, and who performs best under intense pressure. This knowledge, combined with their coaching acumen and the performance of players, can make the difference between losing and winning.

Coaches of individual-player sports, such as track or tennis, usually do most of their coaching in practice before the competition. Athletes must then apply these coaching lessons to competition. During competition, coaches encourage players, offer tips to improve their performance, and take notes on their performance and technique for use in future practices.

Coaches need to be willing to learn new coaching techniques. Many attend clinics or seminars to learn more about their individual sports or how to teach players more effectively. Many coaches are members of professional organizations that deal exclusively with their individual sports.

Coaches should be strong communicators, since they are often interviewed by print, radio, and television reporters. They also make appearances at fund-raisers, fan fests, and other events.

Coaches also must recruit new players. During the off season, college coaches actively recruit new players to join their teams. They travel across the country and even the world to scout promising high school players who might be a good fit for their team. They meet with promising players and their parents and offer scholarships to try to convince these players to attend their college and play for their team.

REQUIREMENTS

High School

To prepare for college, take human physiology, psychology, biology, health, and exercise classes. Courses in English and speech will help you to develop your communication skills. Playing and coaching sports is one of the best ways to learn more about this career while you are in high school. If you can't play or coach sports, volunteer to work as a team statistician, equipment manager, or sports reporter on your school's newspaper. These jobs will allow you to observe coaches at work.

Postsecondary Training

Though there is no standard educational path for aspiring coaches, most college coaches have bachelor's degrees. Some college coaches were student athletes in college, while others attended college and received their degrees without playing a sport. Most college coaches begin their careers at small colleges where teaching is part of their job duties. To become a college teacher, you will need to earn at least a bachelor's degree in education or another subject area.

Other Requirements

To be a successful college coach, you need to be extremely knowledgeable about your sport, including its rules and strategies. You need to be an effective communicator in order to be able to teach your players the fundamentals of your sport, impart game strategies, and encourage team play.

Coaches must be steady, disciplined leaders who are able to patiently instruct players as they practice plays and techniques over and over. They must keep in mind that all athletes learn and improve

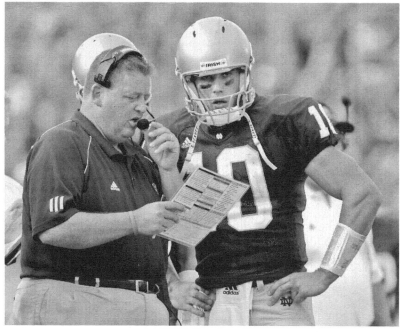

Charlie Weis, head football coach at the University of Notre Dame, discusses strategy with quarterback Brady Quinn during a game. *(John Gress, Reuters, Corbis)*

at different rates. Coaches should be optimistic and have strong motivational skills. They should maintain the same professional demeanor whether they are winning or losing games.

Coaches must be able to work well under pressure as they guide their teams through games and tournaments that carry great personal stakes for everyone involved.

EXPLORING

If you are interested in a career in coaching, get involved with playing and coaching sports as early as possible. Play as many high school sports as you can. Volunteer to assist coaches of Little League baseball, Pop Warner football, or other youth leagues. Work as a counselor or coach at a summer sports camp. Ask your school counselor to set up an interview with a local coach. These activities will help you discover if coaching is something that you enjoy.

You might also consider subscribing to publications such as *Coaching Digest* (baseball, http://www.abca.org), *Basketball Sense* (http://www.basketballsense.com), and *Soccer Journal* (http://www. nscaa.com). These magazines are geared toward coaches, players, and fans who are interested in sports coaching. Visit the Web sites of these organizations to read sample issues and articles.

EMPLOYERS

Most of the two- and four-year colleges and universities in the United States have sports programs that employ sports coaches. Besides working for colleges, coaches are employed by high schools, professional sports teams, individual athletes, youth leagues, summer camps, and recreation centers. After finishing their coaching careers, some college coaches pursue opportunities in broadcasting or work as motivational speakers.

STARTING OUT

Aspiring college coaches often begin their careers by working as high school coaches, youth league coaches, or recreation center coaches. One of the best ways to get coaching experience at the college level is to work as a graduate assistant coach. Graduate assistant coaches are recent graduates who are interested in becoming coaches. They receive a stipend and gain valuable coaching experience assisting head coaches.

ADVANCEMENT

A typical advancement path for a successful coach might be from high school coach, to assistant college coach, to head coach at a junior college, to head coach at a small Division I program. Successful Division I college coaches can advance to become assistant and head coaches for professional sports teams. Some coaches never become head coaches but have fulfilling careers as assistant coaches at the amateur and professional levels.

EARNINGS

The U.S. Department of Labor reports that the mean earnings for sports coaches who worked at colleges and universities were $44,200 in 2006. Salaries for coaches at all levels ranged from less than $13,990 to more than $58,890.

Head college football coaches at NCAA Division I schools earned an average of $950,000 a year in 2006, according to *USA Today*. A few top football coaches earn more than $2 million annually.

Some top coaches in men's Division I basketball earn salaries of $1 million or more, according to *USA Today*. For example, Tubby Smith, men's basketball coach at the University of Kentucky, earned approximately $2.1 million in 2006, while Ohio State's Thad Matta and Michigan State's Tom Izzo earned more than $1.7 million.

Coaches of women's sports typically earn lower salaries than their male colleagues—although top coaches such as Pat Summitt, head coach of the women's basketball team for the University of Tennessee, for example, earn salaries that are on par with coaches of men's basketball teams. In 2006, Summitt earned $1.125 million.

Many popular coaches augment their salaries with income from personal appearances and endorsements.

WORK ENVIRONMENT

College sports coaches work indoors in climate-controlled conditions and outdoors in conditions that range from comfortable to hot, humid, cold, rainy, and snowy. In outdoor stadiums, weather conditions may affect a team's performance.

College teams compete throughout the United States and Canada. They travel by bus, train, or plane to competitions. Players and coaches stay in hotels while on the road.

Many college coaches work part time, with teaching or other activities filling the remainder of their time. Coaches in high-profile college sports such as football and basketball may work year-round. During the sports season, coaches may work up to 16 hours a day, five or six days each week. Games often occur on nights and weekends.

There is very little job security in college coaching. Athletic directors expect their coaches to consistently win, especially in such financially lucrative sports as football and basketball. Coaches are often fired if their teams do not perform up to expectations.

OUTLOOK

Although the U.S. Department of Labor predicts that the occupation of sports coaching will grow faster than the average for all occupations through 2014, the number of college coaching opportunities is not expected to increase. Some colleges have cut less-popular sports programs, which has reduced the number of coaching positions. Openings will be available as coaches retire or are terminated. However, coaches have little job security unless they can consistently produce winning teams.

FOR MORE INFORMATION

For certification information, trade journals, job listings, and a list of graduate schools, visit the AAHPERD Web site.

American Alliance for Health, Physical Education, Recreation and Dance (AAHPERD)
1900 Association Drive
Reston, VA 20191-1598
Tel: 800-213-7193
Email: info@aahperd.org
http://www.aahperd.org

For information on membership and baseball coaching education, coaching Web links, and job listings, visit the ABCA Web site.

American Baseball Coaches Association (ABCA)
108 South University Avenue, Suite 3
Mount Pleasant, MI 48858-2327
Tel: 989-775-3300
Email: abca@abca.org
http://www.abca.org

For information on football coaching careers, contact
American Football Coaches Association
100 Legends Lane
Waco, TX 76706-1243
Tel: 254-754-9900
Email: info@afca.com
http://www.afca.com

For information on hockey coaching, contact
American Hockey Coaches Association
7 Concord Street
Gloucester, MA 01930-2300
Tel: 781-245-4177
http://www.ahcahockey.com

For information on careers in sports and physical education, contact
National Association for Sport and Physical Education
1900 Association Drive
Reston, VA 20191-1598
Tel: 800-213-7193
Email: naspe@aahperd.org
http://www.aahperd.org/naspe

For information on basketball coaching, contact
National Association of Basketball Coaches
1111 Main Street, Suite 1000
Kansas City, MO 64105-2136
Tel: 816-878-6222
http://nabc.ocsn.com

For information on college athletics, contact the following associations
National Association of Intercollegiate Athletics
1200 Grand Boulevard
Kansas City, MO 64106-2304
Tel: 816-595-8000
http://www.naia.org

National Collegiate Athletic Association
PO Box 6222
Indianapolis, IN 46206-6222
Tel: 317-917-6222
http://ncaa.com

For information on the coaching of soccer, contact
National Soccer Coaches Association of America
6700 Squibb Road, Suite 215
Mission, KS 66202-3252
Tel: 800-458-0678
http://www.nscaa.com

For information on women's basketball coaching, contact
Women's Basketball Coaches Association
4646 Lawrenceville Highway
Lilburn, GA 30047-3620
Tel: 770-279-8027
Email: wbca@wbca.org
http://www.wbca.org

Diet and Fitness Writers

QUICK FACTS

School Subjects
English
Health
Physical education

Personal Skills
Communication/ideas
Helping/teaching

Work Environment
Primarily indoors
Primarily one location

Minimum Education Level
Bachelor's degree

Salary Range
$25,430 to $48,640 to
$97,700+

Certification or Licensing
None available

Outlook
About as fast as the average

DOT
131

GOE
01.02.01

NOC
5121

O*NET-SOC
27-3043.00

OVERVIEW

Diet and fitness writers express, edit, promote, and interpret ideas and facts about nutrition and exercise in written form for books, magazines, Web sites, trade journals, newspapers, technical studies and reports, and company newsletters.

These writers may report on their own experiences, or they may write about the diet or sports activities of others. Some diet and fitness writers create articles or full books on new dieting methods or exercise forms to persuade the public to adopt the dieting or fitness trend.

HISTORY

Dieting and fitness are important to many people's lives today. But they have not always been on everyone's mind. The word *diet* actually refers to the food that one eats regularly, not a restrictive eating plan. This is why some people are said to have healthy diets, while many others follow poor diets (think fast food, convenience choices, and sugar- and fat-laden treats).

According to diet author Dr. Beth Gruber, one of the first individuals to put a diet into written form was an Englishman named William Banting. In 1850, Banting could hardly walk down the stairs or tie his own shoes because of his weight. In other words, he was obese (though this term had yet to be coined). After trying starvation, diuretics, and extreme exercise with no success, he found Dr. William Harvey, who recommended that Banting eliminate all sugar and starches from his diet. This approach finally brought success, and Banting lost 50 pounds at a safe rate. More importantly, he wrote about his experience, and his pamphlet titled *Letter on Corpulence Addressed to the Public* was read by people in countries around the world. Banting's work became the first written record of a diet that is still popular: the low-carbohydrate diet.

The need and desire to be fit has long been part of the human existence, from primitive man needing to be quick and strong to hunt for food, to the first modern Olympic athletes in 1896 wanting to be quick and strong to win competitions.

In the United States, colonial life was tough enough that simple daily living required a good amount of fitness. According to Lance C. Dalleck and Len Kravitz, Ph.D., authors of *The History of Fitness,* early leaders such as Benjamin Franklin recommended a daily dose of exercise, including running, swimming, and even resistance training. President Thomas Jefferson also promoted the benefits of exercise, though possibly to extremes, recommending no less than two hours a day of physical activity.

Starting with the industrial revolution and continuing on to modern times, many jobs that once required physical effort are now done in part by machines and other forms of technology. As a result, people have become more sedentary, which has increased the need to find forms of exercise outside of physical labor.

One fitness pioneer was Jack LaLanne. In the 1950s, he hosted a successful television program that set the stage for other fitness personalities, such as Jane Fonda and Richard Simmons. LaLanne recommended a program of aerobic movement, either on a floor or in the water, and resistance training using machines with pulleys. He is even credited with inventing the (appropriately named) "jumping jack."

A more recent fitness pioneer is Dr. Ken H. Cooper, who, according to Dalleck and Kravitz, is recognized as the "Father of the Modern Fitness Movement." Cooper emphasizes using fitness not as a treatment course for disease, but as a method of disease prevention. LaLanne and Cooper have spurred many others to write about and promote their own recipes for fitness.

THE JOB

Diet and fitness writers work in the field of communications. Specifically, they deal with the written word, whether it is destined for the printed page, broadcast, or a computer screen. The nature of their work is as varied as the materials they produce. They may write health and fitness articles for books, magazines, and journals. They also contribute to scientific research and technical reports. Many writers promote popular diet or fitness trends, such as the Atkins or Zone diets or the various forms of yoga. They may write advertisement copy or contribute to health and fitness segments for radio and television broadcasts.

Many successful diet and fitness writers have extensive educational or work experience related to their subject matter. However, those with specialized degrees and certifications must be able to communicate clearly with their intended audience. For example, a registered dietitian with an extensive background in biology and chemistry who writes for a general publication must be able to break down highly technical information on food composition into terms the average reader can understand and use.

Diet and fitness writers can be employed either as in-house staff or as freelancers. Pay varies according to experience and position, but freelancers must provide their own office space and equipment such as computers and fax machines. Freelancers also are responsible for keeping tax records, sending out invoices, negotiating contracts, and providing their own health insurance.

REQUIREMENTS

High School
While in high school, build a broad educational foundation by taking courses in English, literature, health, science, computer science, and typing. The ability to type and a familiarity with computers are extremely important if you want to pursue a career in writing.

Postsecondary Training
Competition for writing jobs in the diet and fitness arena is very strong. A college education may not be required, but it helps to establish your skills as a writer. If you want to be hired full time as a diet or fitness writer, employers may prefer that you have a background in nutrition or sports fitness as well as course work in English or journalism. Some highly technical journals or scientific research publications require their writers to have a master's degree.

In addition to formal course work, most employers look for practical writing experience. Experience with high school and college newspapers, yearbooks, and literary magazines will make you a better candidate. In addition, experience with a small community newspaper, radio station, or local television station is also valuable. Many book publishers, magazines, newspapers, and radio and television stations have summer internship programs that provide valuable training if you want to learn about the publishing and broadcasting businesses. Interns do many simple tasks, such as running errands and answering phones, but some may be asked to perform research, conduct interviews, or even write some minor pieces. During these internships, express your interest in writing about health or fitness. That way, if such an assignment comes along, you may be the first to be asked to help.

Certification and Licensing

Many diet and fitness writers also work as personal trainers, dietitians, or nutritionists, or in other related careers. Many of these positions require additional education and certification to advise clients. For example, the American Council on Exercise and American Fitness Professionals and Associates offer various types of certification, depending on your work interests. Individuals may choose to obtain certification as a trainer, nutrition consultant, exercise specialist, or pre/postnatal exercise instructor.

Other Requirements

To be a diet or fitness writer, you should be creative and able to express ideas clearly, have broad and specialized knowledge pertaining to your field of interest, be skilled in research techniques, and be computer literate. Other assets include curiosity, persistence, initiative, resourcefulness, and an accurate memory. For some jobs—on a health and fitness magazine staff, for example, where the activity is hectic and deadlines are short—the ability to concentrate and produce under pressure is essential.

EXPLORING

As a high school or college student, you can test your interest in and aptitude for the writing field by serving as a reporter or writer on school newspapers, yearbooks, and literary magazines. You should also explore the field of fitness and nutrition by participating in sports and taking part in health clinics or workshops.

Small community newspapers, magazines, and newsletters often welcome contributions from outside sources, although they may not have the resources to pay for submissions. Jobs in bookstores, magazine shops, and even newsstands will offer you a chance to become familiar with various publications, including those covering health, dieting, fitness, and sports.

You can also obtain information on writing careers by visiting local newspapers, publishers, or radio and television stations and interviewing some of the writers who work there. Career conferences and other guidance programs frequently include authors of all types from local or national organizations.

EMPLOYERS

Health and fitness writers are employed by newspapers, magazines, and book publishers; advertising agencies and public relations firms; in radio and television broadcasting; and by journals and newsletters published by business and nonprofit organizations, such as the American Dietetic Association and the American Council on Exercise. Other employers include government agencies and Web sites. However, most diet and fitness writers are self-employed, working as freelancers for various magazines, book publishers, and Web sites that focus on health and sports.

STARTING OUT

A fair amount of experience is required to gain a full-time position as a diet and fitness writer. Most writers start out in entry-level positions. These jobs may be listed with college career services offices, or they may be obtained by applying directly to the employment departments of the individual publishers or broadcasting companies. Graduates who previously served internships often have the advantage of knowing someone who can give them a personal recommendation. Want ads in newspapers and trade journals are another source for jobs. Because of the competition for positions, however, few vacancies are listed with public or private employment agencies.

In most cases, employers will want to see your resume as well as samples of your published writing. These samples are often assembled in an organized portfolio or scrapbook. Bylined or signed articles are more credible (and, as a result, more useful) than stories without an identified source.

Beginning positions as a junior staff writer usually involve library research, preparation of rough drafts for part or all of a piece, cataloging, and other related writing tasks. These are generally carried on under the supervision of a more experienced writer or editor.

ADVANCEMENT

Diet and fitness writers may work in other fields full time and write on health or fitness topics in their free time. Once a writer is published, he or she can build a portfolio, gain a reputation as a writer, and possibly move into writing full time. Freelance or self-employed writers earn advancement in the form of larger fees as they gain exposure and establish their reputations.

Other diet or fitness writers find their first jobs as editorial or production assistants. Advancement may be more rapid in small companies, where beginners learn by doing a little bit of everything and may be given specialized writing tasks immediately. In large publishing houses or firms, duties are usually more compartmentalized. Assistants in entry-level positions are assigned such tasks as research, fact checking, and copywriting, and it generally takes much longer to advance to full-scale writing duties.

Promotion into positions of higher responsibility may come with the assignment of more important or specialized articles and stories to write, or it may be the result of moving to another employer. Mobility among employees in this field is common. An assistant in one publishing house may switch to an executive position in another. Or a writer may switch to a related job, such as personal trainer or dietitian, as a type of advancement.

EARNINGS

In 2006, median annual earnings for all salaried writers and authors were $48,640 a year, according to the U.S. Department of Labor. The lowest paid 10 percent earned less than $25,430, while the highest paid 10 percent earned $97,700 or more. In book publishing, some specialties pay better than others.

In addition to their salaries, many writers earn additional income from freelance work. Part-time freelancers may earn from $5,000 to $15,000 a year. Freelance earnings vary widely. Full-time established freelance writers may earn more than $75,000 a year.

WORK ENVIRONMENT

Working conditions vary for writers. Although full-time writers typically work 35 to 40 hours a week, many writers work overtime. A health or fitness publication that is published frequently has more deadlines closer together, creating greater pressures to meet them. The work is especially hectic at newspapers and broadcasting companies, which operate seven days a week. These specialized writers often work nights and weekends to meet deadlines or to cover a last-minute story.

Most writers work independently, but they often must cooperate with artists, photographers, rewriters, and editors who may have widely differing ideas of how the materials should be prepared and presented.

Physical surroundings range from comfortable private offices to noisy, crowded newsrooms filled with other workers typing on their computers and talking on the telephone. Some writers must confine their research to the library or telephone interviews, but others may travel to other cities or countries or to local sites, such as restaurants, sports arenas, health centers, or other offices.

Freelance writers generally work from their own homes. As a result, they need a personal computer, printer, fax machine, copier, and Internet access.

The work can be arduous, but most writers are seldom bored. The most difficult element is the continual pressure of deadlines. People who are the most content as writers enjoy and work well with deadline pressure.

OUTLOOK

The employment of all writers is expected to increase about as fast as the average for all occupations through 2014, according to the U.S. Department of Labor. The demand for writers by newspapers, periodicals, book publishers, and nonprofit organizations is expected to increase. The growth of online publishing will also demand many talented writers; those with computer skills will have an advantage as a result.

The major book and magazine publishers, broadcasting companies, and the federal government account for the concentration of writers in large cities such as New York, Chicago, Los Angeles, Boston, Philadelphia, San Francisco, and Washington, D.C. Opportunities with small newspapers, corporations, and professional, technical, and trade publications can be found throughout the country.

People entering this field should realize that the competition for jobs is extremely keen. Beginners, especially, may have difficulty finding employment. Of the thousands who graduate each year with degrees in English, journalism, communications, and the liberal arts, intending to establish a career as a writer, many turn to other occupations when they find that applicants far outnumber the job openings available. College students would do well to keep this in mind and prepare for a related alternate career in areas such as nutrition or physical education in the event they cannot obtain a position as a diet or fitness writer.

FOR MORE INFORMATION

For general health and fitness topics and to learn about fitness certifications, contact
American Council on Exercise
4851 Paramount Drive
San Diego, CA 92123-1449

Tel: 800-825-3636
Email: support@acefitness.org
http://www.acefitness.org

The ADA is the single best source of information about careers in dietetics. Its Web site is an excellent resource that provides detailed information and links to other organizations and resources.
American Dietetic Association (ADA)
120 South Riverside Plaza, Suite 2000
Chicago, IL 60606-6995
Tel: 800-877-1600
http://www.eatright.org

For information on home study and various fitness certifications, contact
American Fitness Professionals and Associates
PO Box 214
Ship Bottom, NJ 08008-0234
Tel: 609-978-7583
Email: afpa@afpafitness.com
http://www.afpafitness.com

For educational and career information, contact
American Society for Nutrition
9650 Rockville Pike, Suite L-4500
Bethesda, MD 20814-3998
Tel: 301-634-7050
Email: info@nutrition.org
http://www.asns.org

For general educational information on all areas of journalism, including newspapers, magazines, television, and radio, contact
Association for Education in Journalism and Mass
    Communication
234 Outlet Pointe Boulevard
Columbia, SC 29210-5667
Tel: 803-798-0271
http://www.aejmc.org

Dietitians and Nutritionists

OVERVIEW

Registered dietitians (RDs) are professionals who have met certain educational requirements and passed a national certification exam. For the purposes of this article, the terms *dietitian* and *registered dietitian* will be used interchangeably. RDs provide people with foods and dietary advice that will improve or maintain their health. They may be self-employed or work for institutions, such as hospitals, schools, restaurants, and nursing homes—any place where food is served or nutritional counseling is required. *Hospital dietitians,* for example, may ensure that the food served in the cafeteria is nourishing or create special diets for patients with particular nutritional problems and needs.

Regulation of those using the professional title nutritionist varies by state. For example, in some states a person without any specialized training may be able to call himself or herself a nutritionist and offer dietary advice. For the purposes of this article, however, the term *nutritionist* refers to *certified clinical nutritionists* (CCNs) who have received specialized training and passed a certification exam. CCNs usually work in private practice and are concerned with the biochemical aspects of nutrition.

There are approximately 50,000 dietitians and nutritionists working in the United States.

HISTORY

Nutrition has been an important concern to people throughout the world for millennia, and the use of food as medicine has been recognized throughout recorded history. In India, the form of medicine known as Ayurveda, which tailors diets to individuals to cure or to maintain health, has been practiced for as long as 5,000 years. Traditional Chinese medicine, which is approximately as old as Ayurveda, makes use of many dietary recommendations and proscriptions. Both forms of medicine are still widely used in their countries of origin, and both have spread to other parts of the world.

In ancient Greece, philosophers and healers noted the connection between diet and health, and ultimately it was the Greek practice of careful observation and research that gave rise to the scientific method, on which modern Western nutrition is based. It should be understood, however, that observation and research were also important parts of virtually all other medical traditions.

A major breakthrough in nutrition occurred in the 18th century, when the French chemist Antoine-Laurent Lavoisier began to study the way the body uses food energy, or calories. He also examined the relationship between heat production and the use of energy, and his work has caused him to be known as the "father of nutrition."

By the early 20th century, vitamins had been studied, and the relationship between diets and certain illnesses came to be understood. By 1940, most vitamins and minerals had been discovered and studied, and the field of nutrition had made tremendous strides. Since that time, advances in technology have enabled scientists to learn far more about nutrition than was possible earlier. At present, much is known, but much remains to be learned. It often happens that one study contradicts another regarding the benefits or dangers of certain foods.

THE JOB

Registered dietitians have a broad-based knowledge of foods, dietetics, and food service. They have at least a bachelor's degree in food science or related field from a school accredited by the Commission on Accreditation for Dietetics Education (CADE); they have completed a CADE-accredited internship; and they have passed a registration exam. The term *nutritionist* can refer to a variety of people because regulations covering the use of this title vary from state to state. In some states, anyone—even those with little or no specialized education or credentials—can set up shop as a nutritionist. For the purposes of this article, however, *nutritionists* refers to certified clinical nutritionists. CCNs have the same core educational and internship backgrounds as RDs. In addition, CCNs are specialists who have completed a certain amount of postgraduate education that focuses on the biochemical and physiological aspects of nutrition science.

There are many areas of practice within the rapidly growing and changing field of nutrition. One reason for this growth is that the public has become more aware of the importance of nutrition in recent years, and this development has opened up new areas for dietitians and nutritionists. The list of specialties that follows is by no means exhaustive.

Clinical dietitians are in charge of planning and supervising the preparation of diets designed for specific patients, and they work for such institutions as hospitals and retirement homes. In many cases, their patients cannot eat certain foods for medical reasons, such as diabetes or liver failure, and the dietitians must see that these patients receive nourishing meals. Clinical dietitians work closely with doctors, who advise them regarding the patients' health and the foods that the patients cannot eat. It is often part of a clinical dietitian's job to educate patients about nutritional principles.

Community dietitians usually work for clinics, government health programs, social service agencies, or similar organizations. They counsel individuals or advise the members of certain groups—such as the elderly, families, and pregnant women—regarding nutritional problems, proper eating, and sensible grocery shopping.

Although most dietitians do some kind of teaching in the course of their work, *teaching dietitians* specialize in education. They usually work for hospitals, and they may teach full time or part time. Sometimes teaching dietitians also perform other tasks, such as running a food-service operation, especially in small colleges. In larger institutions, however, those tasks are generally performed by different people. In some cases, teaching dietitians also perform research.

There are many kinds of *consultant dietitians,* who work for such organizations as schools, restaurants, grocery store chains, manufacturers of food-service equipment, pharmaceutical companies, and private companies of various kinds. Some of these organizations have home economics departments that need the services of dietitians. Some consultants spend much of their time advising individuals rather than organizations. One lucrative area for consultants is working with athletes and sports teams, helping to maximize athletes' performance and extend the length of their careers.

Administrative dietitians, also known as *management dietitians,* combine management skills with people skills to organize and run large-scale food operations. They may work for food-service companies, oversee the cafeterias of large corporations, be employed by prisons, or work at long-term-care facilities—basically they work for any organization that provides food services to a large number of people. In addition to planning menus, these dietitians are responsible for such things as creating budgets, drawing up work policies, and enforcing institutional and government regulations related to safety and sanitation.

Research dietitians typically work for government organizations, universities, hospitals, pharmaceutical companies, and manufacturers, and they may specialize in any of a vast number of research subjects. They often work on improving existing food products or finding alternatives to foods that are unhealthy when eaten in substantial portions.

Certified clinical nutritionists typically work in private practice for themselves, as part of a group of health care professionals, or for a doctor or doctors in private practice. CCNs are specialists who have completed at least some post-graduate training in nutrition science. They work with clients to correct imbalances in the clients' biochemistry and improve their physiological function. Through lab tests, consultations with doctors, and discussions with the clients themselves, CCNs review the clients' overall health and lifestyle and determine what nutrients the clients have too little or too much of. They then come up with plans to enable their clients to get the correct nutrition in order to get their bodies back into balance. Their clients may range from people who are slightly ill, for example, or those who feel run down all the time but do not know why, to people with serious diseases, such as heart disease or cancers. No matter what problem brings a client to a CCN, though, the CCN's goal is to correct that client's biochemistry in order to help that person feel better.

REQUIREMENTS

High School

If you want to be a dietitian or a nutritionist, you should take as many courses as possible in health, biology, chemistry, family and consumer science, and mathematics. If you are not sufficiently prepared in high school, you are likely to struggle with such college courses as mathematics and biochemistry. Communication skills are also important, since dietitians and nutritionists must interact effectively with clients, employers, and colleagues. Even researchers who spend most of their time in the lab must cooperate with colleagues and write clear, accurate reports on the results of their work.

For this reason, dietitians and nutritionists must be well versed in spoken and written English. Psychology, which generally is taught in college nutrition programs, is an important aspect of the work of many dietitians and nutritionists.

Postsecondary Training

There are a couple different educational routes you can choose from to become a dietitian. The first is to complete a bachelor's or master's level CADE-accredited coordinated program that combines classroom work with 900 hours of supervised internship experience. Currently there are more than 50 programs of this type. Once you have graduated, you are eligible to take the registration exam. Another option is to get at least your bachelor's degree from a CADE-accredited program that provides only classroom instruction. As of 2004, there were about 227 bachelor's and master's degree programs with CADE accreditation. After receiving your degree you then need to get 900 hours of hands-on experience through a CADE-accredited practice program or internship. Currently there are 265 accredited internship programs, which take six to 24 months to complete (depending on whether you are on a full- or part-time schedule). Once you have completed both of these steps, you are eligible to take the registration exam. The American Dietetic Association (ADA) notes that there is no list of courses all would-be dietitians should take. However, the ADA does provide the *Directory of Dietetic Programs* of selected programs that meet CADE standards. In addition, the ADA Web site (http://www.eatright.org/cade) also provides a listing of these schools. Those who enter this field typically get degrees in food and nutrition science, dietetics, food service, or other related areas. Course work may include classes in economics, business management, culinary arts, biochemistry, physiology, and food science. If you want to teach, do research, or work in public health, you should get a bachelor's degree and one or more advanced degrees.

Nutritionists complete the same type of undergraduate education as dietitians, including fulfilling the 900 hours of a supervised internship. They must also complete at minimum a certain number of courses at the master's degree level to be eligible to sit for the clinical nutritionist certification exam. Many actually complete a master's or Ph.D. in nutrition science.

Certification or Licensing

Currently 46 states have laws regulating the practice of dietitians and nutritionists through licensure, certification, or registration. Of these states, 31 require licensure, 14 require certification, and one requires registration.

The registered dietitian (RD) credential is awarded by the Commission on Dietetic Registration of the ADA. To receive this designation, dietitians must have completed CADE-approved education and training and pass the registration exam. To maintain their standing, registered dietitians must also complete continuing education on a regular basis. Some specialty certifications, such as board certified specialist in pediatric nutrition and board certified specialist in sports dietetics, are also available through the ADA.

The CCN credential is awarded by the Clinical Nutrition Certification Board of the International and American Associations of Clinical Nutritionists. To receive this designation, nutritionists must have completed a bachelor's degree (which includes certain classes in the sciences and nutrition), done post-graduate studies in clinical nutrition, finished an internship, and passed the written examination. Recertification is required every five years.

Other Requirements

Because there are so many technical requirements in the field of nutrition, dietitians and nutritionists must be detail oriented and able to think analytically. Math and science are a major part of both training and work. Dietitians and nutritionists must be comfortable making decisions and acting on them. Even those who do not work as consultants have to be disciplined and decisive.

For most dietitians, flexibility is crucial. Karen Petty, RD, an administrator who began her career as a clinical dietitian, says about working in institutional food service: "You will never be able to please everyone, because everyone has different tastes in food. You learn to be able to take criticism and go on to try to please the majority."

People who want to become administrators must have people skills. On that subject, Petty says: "When I'm asked what is the hardest part of my job, I never hesitate to say it's personnel management." For administrators, the ability to communicate clearly and effectively is particularly important.

EXPLORING

You can start exploring this type of work right in your own kitchen. Learn healthy ways to cook and bake. Plan and prepare meals for your family; do your own grocery shopping and learn to pick out the best produce, meats, fish, and other ingredients. In addition to taking family and consumer science classes at school, take cooking classes offered by other organizations in your community. Supermarkets, for example, frequently offer classes on topics such as how to prepare low cholesterol meals. Another option is to contact dietitians and nutritionists and ask them about their work. School cafeterias, local hospitals, and nursing homes are all places to look for those who would be willing to have an information interview with you. And, of course, one of the best ways to learn about nutrition is to get a job in a food-related business such as a restaurant or a hospital cafeteria. In such a setting, you will be able to observe and interact with dietitians as they work.

EMPLOYERS

Approximately 50,000 dietitians and nutritionists are employed in the United States. Many kinds of government and private organizations hire dietitians, and the kinds of available opportunities continue to increase. There are opportunities in hospitals, schools of all levels, community health programs, day care centers, correctional facilities, health clubs, weight-management clinics, health management organizations, nursing homes, government organizations, food-service companies, food equipment manufacturers, sports teams, pharmaceutical companies, and grocery store chains, to name a few. Among the large organizations that need dietitians are the armed forces, which have to feed their personnel as well and as inexpensively as possible. In addition, dietitians and nutritionists can work in private practice, running their own consulting businesses or working in a group practice.

STARTING OUT

Because dietitians and nutritionists are extensively trained and have some practical experience before they look for their first job, they tend to know the type of organization they want to work for. Most colleges and universities provide placement services, and people often find work through connections they make at school or in practice programs. For this reason, it is wise to make as many professional connections as possible.

Some parts of the country have more dietitians and nutritionists than others, and beginning dietitians should consider taking positions out of their areas in order to get started in the business. Jobs can be found via trade journals, national and state conventions, Web sites, classified ads, and specialized employment agencies. Although it is possible to call organizations to learn about job opportunities, the most effective way to find work is through personal contacts.

ADVANCEMENT

There are various ways to advance in the business. One of the best is further education. RDs with only a bachelor's degree may wish to obtain an advanced degree, which will enable them to apply for research, teaching, or public health positions that are not otherwise open to them. For example, a dietitian interested in working in community dietetics may get an advanced degree in public health; someone wanting to move into management may get a master's in business administration. RDs can also advance by getting further education that leads to specialty certification, such as the CCN or the CSP. Often advancement depends upon the goals of the individual, as he or she decides where to go with this career.

In the field of nutrition, as in most others, seniority, reliability, expertise, and experience count. An experienced clinical dietitian might ultimately become an administrative dietitian, for example, and a research dietitian might take charge of a research department.

EARNINGS

Salaries vary by practice area, years of experience, educational level, and location. In general, administrative, self-employed, and business dietitians earn more than their clinical and community counterparts.

According to the U.S. Department of Labor, the median annual salary for dietitians and nutritionists was $46,980 in 2006. The lowest paid 10 percent earned less than $29,860; the highest paid 10 percent earned more than $68,330 a year.

The ADA reports findings from its membership indicate that of dietitians employed for five years or less, 50 percent had yearly earnings of $35,000 to $46,000. The ADA also found that RDs in business, private practice, and consulting earned more than $72,000 per year.

Benefits such as health insurance, sick pay, paid vacations and holidays, and 401(k) plans are as prevalent in the field of nutrition as they are in other fields. Naturally, dietitians who run their own businesses must make their own arrangements in these areas.

WORK ENVIRONMENT

Nutritionists usually work in medical office settings that are clean, well lit, and organized. Dietitians generally work in offices or kitchens. Such environments are usually clean and well lit, although some kitchens may be hot and stifling. Some dietitians and nutritionists sit much of the time, while others spend all day on their feet. Most

Mean Annual Earnings by Specialty, 2006

Federal government	$61,690
Home health care services	$55,470
Scientific research and development services	$52,570
Outpatient care centers	$51,240
General medical and surgical hospitals	$48,220
State government	$47,630
Nursing care facilities	$47,110
Local government	$44,420

Source: U.S. Department of Labor

work 40-hour weeks, but some—especially dietitians who work for hospitals and restaurants—are required to work on weekends and at odd hours. Part-time positions are also common.

Some hospitals offer dietitians room, board, and laundry services for a nominal fee, but this arrangement is becoming less common. In the past, many college dietitians lived in apartments provided by the school, but this arrangement is also becoming a thing of the past, except where dietitians run food-service operations in residence halls.

OUTLOOK

According to the U.S. Department of Labor, employment of dietitians and nutritionists will grow faster than the average for all occupations through 2014. One contributing factor to continued growth is the public's increasing awareness of the importance of nutrition. Another is the fact that the average age of the population is increasing rapidly, which will bring about a growing need for nutritional counseling and planning in hospitals, residential care facilities, schools, prisons, community health programs, and home health care agencies. Opportunities will also be good for dietitians and nutritionists who work for contract providers of food services, in outpatient care centers, and in offices of physicians and other health care professionals. Workers who are employed in hospitals and nursing homes that hire contractors to handle food-service operations will have less promising employment prospects.

FOR MORE INFORMATION

The ADA is the single best source of information about careers in dietetics. Its Web site is an excellent resource that provides detailed information and links to other organizations and resources.
American Dietetic Association (ADA)
120 South Riverside Plaza, Suite 2000
Chicago, IL 60606-6995
Tel: 800-877-1600
Email: education@eatright.org
http://www.eatright.org

The goal of the ASN is to improve people's quality of life through the nutritional sciences. It is a good source of educational and career information.
American Society for Nutrition (ASN)
9650 Rockville Pike, Suite L-4500
Bethesda, MD 20814-3998
Tel: 301-634-7050
Email: info@nutrition.org
http://www.asns.org

For information on dietitian certification, contact
Commission on Dietetic Registration
120 South Riverside Plaza, Suite 2000
Chicago, IL 60606-6995
Tel: 800-877-1600, ext. 5500
Email: cdr@eatright.org
http://www.cdrnet.org

For more information on becoming a certified clinical nutritionist, contact
International and American Associations of Clinical Nutritionists
15280 Addison Road, Suite 130
Addison, TX 75001-4551
Tel: 972- 407-9089
Email: ddc@clinicalnutrition.com
http://www.iaacn.org

Exercise Physiologists

QUICK FACTS

School Subjects
Health
Physical education

Personal Skills
Communication/ideas
Helping/teaching

Work Environment
Primarily indoors
Primarily one location

Minimum Education Level
Bachelor's degree

Salary Range
$25,000 to $37,000 to
$60,000+

Certification or Licensing
Recommended

Outlook
Faster than the average

DOT
076

GOE
N/A

NOC
4167

O*NET-SOC
N/A

OVERVIEW

Exercise is not just for the young and healthy. Today, it is prescribed as a way to help people recover from chronic illness, surgery, and injury. *Exercise physiologists* use their knowledge and training of exercise science to help patients reach optimum health, mobility, and confidence. Exercise physiologists work in clinical settings such as hospitals, nursing homes, and rehabilitation centers. They may also be employed by sports-related businesses such as health and fitness clubs or athletic training facilities and camps. Some choose to work in academia.

HISTORY

Humanity has been aware of the integral relationship between exercise and health for thousands of years. More than two thousand years ago, Hippocrates, the Greek physician who is recognized as the father of medicine stated: "If we could give every individual the right amount of nourishment and exercise, not too little and not too much, we would have found the safest way to health."

It was not until the late 1800s, however, that the concepts of exercise physiology began to be studied in depth in the United States. Dr. Dudley Allen Sargent was a pioneer in physical education at Harvard University, and created the Sargent School of Physical Training at the university in 1881. He developed a system for physical examination that included strength testing and anthropometric measures. His vertical jump test, known as the Sargent Test, is still used today.

Many cite the creation of the Harvard Fatigue Laboratory in 1927 as a key event in the development of exercise physiology in the United

States. The laboratory, which closed in 1947, conducted ground-breaking research in exercise and environmental physiology—much of which is still used today.

In the following decades several professional associations (such as the American College of Sports Medicine) were founded to represent exercise science professionals, but it was not until 1997 that an association was created that represented the specific interests of exercise physiologists. The American Society of Exercise Physiologists (ASEP) aims to improve the field of exercise physiology through certification, visibility, and professionalism.

THE JOB

Exercise physiologists may work in a clinical setting such as a hospital, rehabilitation center, or nursing home, where their client base may range from patients recovering from a recent heart attack to coping with chronic arthritis. Their first step in treatment is conducting a thorough patient assessment, which consists of a patient interview and fitness test. Exercise physiologists may have the patient walk on a treadmill while connected to an EKG machine. The EKG machine monitors the patient's heart rate and rhythm to ensure it remains within a safe range. Exercise physiologists may check the patient's blood pressure during the fitness tests to monitor their response to exercise. Patients may also be asked to wear a pulse oximeter on their finger; this device measures the concentration of oxygen in their blood. Other tools such as weights, bands, and balls may also be used to test for strength and flexibility.

After gathering test results, the exercise physiologist confers with the patient's doctors before creating a care plan. He or she will choose exercises to help patients meet specific goals and schedule the number of sessions needed. Cardiac conditioning exercises may be prescribed to increase lung capacity for those suffering from lung disease, or to strengthen the heart of an individual who is recovering from a heart attack. A plan of action could include sessions on the treadmill, stationary bikes, or stairs, as well as weight training with small free weights or bands. The exercise physiologist carefully monitors patients during workout sessions, keeping watch for rapid changes in heart rate, fatigue, or other adverse reactions. They also give the patient constant encouragement and evaluate their progress. Care plans may be altered to increase or decrease activity as tolerated by the patient. The exercise physiologist charts all results and shares this report with the patient and the patient's physicians.

Exercise physiologists working in the fitness industry or athletic training follow the same routine as those working in clinical settings. Personal evaluation is done to identify the client's goals. Is the client interested in weight loss, strength training, improving his or her speed and agility, or injury recovery? The exercise physiologist will then create a care plan and exercise routine. They may advise use of weight machines, swimming, massage, muscle manipulation, and nutrition to achieve these goals. Some correctional or service industries may also consult with exercise physiologists. They may suggest special job-related drills such as stair sprints with weights to help firefighters reach optimum conditioning.

It's important for exercise physiologists to stay abreast of new developments in their field, be it nutritional advances, or new exercise techniques and equipment. The ASEP offers continuing education opportunities as well as a certification program for qualified candidates.

REQUIREMENTS

High School

Students interested in a career in exercise physiology can begin to prepare themselves by taking relevant classes while in high school. Classes such as anatomy, physiology, and biology can give you insight on how the muscles and skeletal structure of the body work together for movement and control. Classes in nutrition and health will provide background on how food and exercise play a vital role in the body's well being.

Postsecondary Training

In today's competitive world, having a master's degree in exercise physiology or exercise science is almost a requirement for the best jobs. In some work settings, such as academia, a Ph.D. is the norm. Some students study exercise physiology as a solid foundation for further education in physical therapy, medicine, dentistry, pharmacy, or chiropractic study. Programs in exercise physiology and exercise science are located throughout the United States. Some suggested elective courses include kinesiology, sport psychology, nutrition and sport, as well as athletic training.

While there are many two- and four-year programs in exercise physiology, only five are accredited by the American Society of Exercise Physiology: Bloomsburg University (Bloomsburg, Pa.), Marquette University (Marquette, Wisc.), the University of New Mexico–Albuquerque, The College of St. Scholastica (Duluth, Minn.), and Slippery Rock University (Slippery Rock, Pa.).

Certification or Licensing
The American Society of Exercise Physiologists offers voluntary board certification to exercise physiologists who have an academic degree in exercise physiology or exercise science (or an academic degree with a concentration in one of the aforementioned majors), pass a written and applied examination, show documentation of a minimum of 400 hours of hands-on laboratory and/or internship experiences in exercise physiology (or related sciences), and meet other requirements.

The American College of Sports Medicine offers professional registration to clinical exercise physiologists who have earned a master's degree in exercise science, movement science, exercise physiology, or kinesiology; passed an examination; accumulated at least 600 hours of clinical experience; and satisfied other requirements. Exercise physiologists who perform exercise testing and train clients with cardiovascular, pulmonary or metabolic diseases can earn the exercise specialist designation.

Some employers may require that exercise physiologists be certified in CPR or as a basic life support provider.

Other Requirements
Exercise physiologists must be experts regarding fitness and health. They must know the appropriate exercise prescription for each physical ailment—from arthritis and asthma to fibromyalgia and congestive heart disease. They must have keen observation skills in order to assess the physical health and fitness progress of their patients. Exercise physiologists also need outgoing personalities since they interact closely with their patients, as well as physicians and other health care professionals. They must know how to motivate and inspire their patients—many of whom may be afraid to begin an exercise regime after a serious illness or injury or who are simply uninterested in exercising.

EXPLORING
Get involved in athletics, whether it be a team or individual sport. There are a host of sports teams available to both males and females at most high schools, ranging from swim team and soccer to basketball and cross-country. Exercise as much as possible, and consider joining a local health club. How can you become an exercise physiologist without believing and practicing in the power of exercise?

Ask your physical education or health teacher to arrange an information interview with an exercise physiologist. Try to get a part-time job at a health club or even with an exercise physiologist working in private practice.

Books to Read

Ehrman, Jonathan. *Clinical Exercise Physiology*. Champaign, Ill.: Human Kinetics Publishers, 2003.

Housh, Terry J., Dona J. Housh, and Herbert A. DeVries. *Applied Exercise and Sport Physiology*. 2d ed. Scottsdale, Ariz.: Holcomb Hathaway, Publishers, 2006.

McArdle, William D., Frank I. Katch, and Victor L. Katch. *Essentials of Exercise Physiology*. 3d ed. Philadelphia: Lippincott Williams & Wilkins, 2005.

Powers, Scott K., and Edward T. Howley. *Exercise Physiology: Theory and Application to Fitness and Performance*. 6th ed. New York: McGraw-Hill Humanities/Social Sciences/Languages, 2006.

Rowland, Thomas W. *Children's Exercise Physiology*. 2d ed. Champaign, Ill.: Human Kinetics Publishers, 2004.

Wilmore, Jack H. *Physiology of Sport and Exercise*. 4th ed. Champaign, Ill.: Human Kinetics Publishers, 2007.

EMPLOYERS

Potential employers will depend on your specialization. Clinical exercise physiologists often work at hospitals, clinics, rehabilitation centers, and nursing homes. Exercise physiologists specializing in sports medicine work with sports and athletic programs of local high schools, colleges and universities, and even professional sports teams. Fitness centers and health clubs are common employers for those working as personal trainers and fitness instructors. Some larger corporations value the importance of exercise and healthy living and contract professionals to design and implement corporate wellness programs for their employees. Those with advanced degrees may find employment at the collegiate level teaching exercise physiology, exercise science, or other related fields.

STARTING OUT

Those with a bachelor's degree will be able to find employment as an exercise physiologist—however, their choices may be limited. A common starting point may be as an assistant to a wellness program director, sports consultant, or physical therapy assistant. Professors of exercise physiology may hire new graduates as research assistants.

An internship will provide you with relevant work experience as well as employment contacts. Some students opt to schedule their internships after graduation; some programs require a semester internship as part of the curriculum. There are many types of internships available in a variety of specialties. For example, the Frankford Hospital Wellness/Nutrition Centers in Philadelphia offer interns a chance to work alongside professionals in different departments such as Cardiac Rehab, Wellness and Nutrition, and Aerobic Coordinator. The Special Olympics in North Carolina also offers an internship program. Here students can apply their education in exercise physiology as well as their organizational skills while helping to prepare and manage the many events of the Special Olympics.

ADVANCEMENT

Exercise physiologists who work at hospitals, clinics, rehabilitation centers, and other clinical settings may advance by becoming managers of teams of exercise physiologists or moving to facilities that are larger or more prestigious. Those who work in educational settings may advance by being assigned additional responsibilities and managerial tasks or moving on to larger schools. Exercise physiologists employed by postsecondary institutions advance in academic rank and may eventually head their departments. Self-employed exercise physiologists advance by attracting more clients or expanding the size of their businesses.

EARNINGS

The U.S. Department of Labor does not provide salary information for the career of exercise physiologist, but according to industry experts, exercise physiologists earn the following salaries based on level of education: bachelor's degree, $25,000 to $32,000; master's degree, $28,000 to $37,000; doctorate, $30,000 to $60,000 or more. Salary.com reports that exercise physiologists earned salaries that ranged from less than $32,852 to $53,266 or more in 2007.

Benefits vary widely depending on the employer but generally include paid holidays and vacations, health insurance, and pension plans.

WORK ENVIRONMENT

Exercise physiologists work in a variety of settings, each dependent on their specialty. Clinics, hospitals, and other healthcare facilities often have brightly lit, comfortable rooms designated for physical therapy or rehabilitation exercises. Some clinical sessions may take place within the patient's private hospital or nursing home room, especially if the patient is too weak for transport. Exercise physiologists may also have an office or cubicle in which to create care plans or do charting. Therapy sessions usually are scheduled during the workweek with a typical 9-to-5 schedule, but some facilities may offer rehab therapy during weekends or in the evenings.

Exercise physiologists specializing in wellness and fitness care work in spacious fitness centers or health clubs. Their hours vary throughout the day and week as determined by the needs of their clients. Those employed at corporate-operated wellness centers may work in facilities that feature the latest cardiovascular and weight training equipment, running track, and swimming pool. Corporate exercise physiologists may also maintain an office within the fitness center for individual consultations. Work hours vary from company to company.

Those employed in academic settings often have a private office. Their classes may take place in a tiny classroom or a large lecture hall, depending on class size, or at times may even take place in the school's gymnasium or fitness center. Their hours vary depending on their class load. Exercise physiology professors spend many additional hours planning lessons and lectures, as well as grading students' coursework and exams.

OUTLOOK

Employment in the fitness and health industries will continue to be strong as exercise is increasingly used to improve health and treat or prevent illness and injury. The U.S. Department of Labor predicts that while opportunities will be good in the near future, competition will increase for the best positions as more and more people enter this relatively new and interesting field. Exercise physiologists with master's degrees and certification will have the best employment opportunities.

FOR MORE INFORMATION

For information on certification, contact
American College of Sports Medicine
PO Box 1440
Indianapolis, IN 46206-1440
Tel: 317-637-9200
http://www.acsm.org

For information on general health and fitness, contact
American Council on Exercise
4851 Paramount Drive
San Diego, CA 92123-1449

Tel: 800-825-3636
Email: support@acefitness.org
http://www.acefitness.org

Visit the society's Web site for profiles of exercise physiologists.
American Physiological Society
9650 Rockville Pike
Bethesda, MD 20814-3991
Tel: 301-634-7164
http://www.the-aps.org

For information on careers and certification, contact
American Society of Exercise Physiologists
c/o The College of St. Scholastica
1200 Kenwood Avenue
Duluth, MN 55811-4199
Tel: 218-723-6297
http://www.asep.org

For information on exercise physiology and to read sample articles from the Journal of Professional Exercise Physiology, *visit the following Web site*
The Center for Exercise Physiology
http://www.exercisephysiologists.com

Fitness Directors

QUICK FACTS

School Subjects
Health
Physical education

Personal Skills
Communication/ideas
Helping/teaching

Work Environment
Primarily indoors
Primarily multiple locations

Minimum Education Level
Some postsecondary training

Salary Range
$18,000 to $32,800 to
$60,000+

Certification or Licensing
Voluntary

Outlook
Much faster than the average

DOT
N/A

GOE
11.01.01

NOC
0513

O*NET-SOC
39-1021.00

OVERVIEW

Fitness directors organize and schedule exercise classes and programs for health clubs, resorts, cruise lines, corporations, and other institutions. They work with other fitness professionals, such as personal trainers, nutritionists, and health care personnel, to deliver the best services for the individuals who use the fitness facility. Fitness directors must balance the needs of their staff with the needs of the paying customers. To do this, directors listen to suggestions from staff and clients regarding program changes or additions, instructor criticisms, and any other comments to make sure the fitness facility runs smoothly and paying customers are happy.

HISTORY

Ask most people what they would like to change about their lifestyle, and many of them will answer, "to exercise more and get in better shape." The desire to be fit is not a recent development, but there are many more options available today than ever in the past.

The fitness industry has seen many changes. Not so long ago, men worked out by pumping iron in their basements, while women were more prone to working out in front of a television to the likes of Jane Fonda. Now, you can work out by going to a spa for an aerobics class and facial all in one day. Exercise is no longer simply something you have to do alone in your basement or in a sweaty, smelly gym. Today, people have options to get in shape. You can work out while on vacation, during your lunch hour in your office building, between classes at school, or even, for the young, at your local daycare center. Fitness has become more accessible and easier to incorporate into our busy work and social lives.

In addition, expanded fitness programming is appealing to a larger audience than before. Programming used to be dominated by floor aerobics. Now, you can take a class in urban dance, Spinning (cycling), or Body Pump (weight lifting). All of these options are possible because of the hard work and organizational skills of fitness directors.

THE JOB

Fitness directors are a crucial part of sports and health facilities. They coordinate the schedules of exercise instructors and personal trainers. They also make sure that their institution offers a wide variety of options to keep customers happy. For example, a fitness director who works at a nursing home must plan and direct classes that appeal to an older population. This director ensures that instructors have experience working with the elderly and then arranges for a class that is low-impact or held in a swimming pool. Exercise classes can be held even while clients remain seated.

On a cruise ship, fitness directors must cater to a wide variety of clients. There may be children on board who would enjoy exercising through games while their parents might enjoy a step aerobics class to help counter all the food eaten that day at the buffet. This balancing act can be a large part of the fitness director's job.

In addition to planning class schedules, directors oversee the overall operation of the fitness facility, making sure equipment and rooms are clean, exercise machines are operating correctly, and the temperature of rooms is comfortable.

Directors must also be observant and make improvements to the programming schedule. For example, perhaps a water aerobics class has not been well attended and is taking up unnecessary lanes in the pool. The facility's fitness director, after talking to lap swimmers that exercise at that time, might decide to eliminate or move the water aerobics class to another time slot, or simply reserve fewer lanes for the class. These are the types of adjustments that directors make on a monthly, if not weekly, basis to keep customers happy.

Because many clients may feel uncomfortable making suggestions or complaints about a class directly to an instructor, fitness directors also serve as a sounding board. Perhaps during an aerobics class, participants are having a hard time hearing the instructor over the music. In this case, a class member can bring the complaint to the attention of the fitness director, who in turn might provide the instructor with a cordless microphone to use during class. Fitness directors keep the peace in health and sports facilities and, as a result, help to keep the facilities in business.

REQUIREMENTS

High School

If you are interested in working in a health and fitness facility, take science and physical education classes and get involved in sports activities. It is also important to take home economics classes, which include lessons in diet and nutrition. Business courses can help you prepare for the management aspect of the job.

Postsecondary Training

Fitness directors should have a background in exercise science to be able to serve their clients and understand the needs of their fitness facility. Associate's and bachelor's degree programs in health education, exercise and sports science, fitness program management, and athletic training are offered in colleges all over the country. Typical classes include nutrition education and consulting, anatomy and physiology, business management, biochemistry, and kinesiology. Because the job of fitness director is a higher management position, most employers will require a bachelor's degree in a sports fitness field and many years of experience in the fitness industry.

Certification or Licensing

Certification in fitness or exercise science is highly recommended (if not required) to work in a management-level position at a fitness facility. Because there are many kinds of certification available, you should choose a certifying board that offers scientifically based exams and requires continuing education credits. The American Council on Exercise and the American Fitness Professionals and Associates are just two of the many organizations with certification programs. Some employers also require that their fitness staff members be certified in cardiopulmonary resuscitation (CPR).

Other Requirements

Fitness directors not only need to know about the industry in which they work, but they also have to be comfortable with managing staff. This requires organization, flexibility, and strong communication skills. A friendly disposition and good people skills are also essential.

EXPLORING

To explore this career, be sure to get fit yourself! If your school offers exercise classes or some other after-school fitness program, sign up and note what you like and dislike about instructor methods or the environment. If there is an affordable gym or health club in your community, take a tour and even a sample class or two. Some clubs offer guest passes for a small fee so prospective members can try out a facility before committing to a membership.

While at the facility, talk to an instructor, manager, or trainer about his or her job and work environment and how to best break into the industry. This way, you can learn about what goes into developing, running, and maintaining a fitness program.

You may even be able to obtain a part-time job at your school or community recreation and fitness center. This would give you the chance to see if you enjoy working in fitness.

EMPLOYERS

Fitness directors work in health clubs, gyms, corporate fitness centers, day care centers, nursing homes, hospitals, rehabilitation centers, resorts, and even for cruise lines. Health and sports centers are located in urban, suburban, and rural areas all over the country.

STARTING OUT

Most fitness directors start out in another career within the sports, health care, or fitness industries. They may start out as personal trainers, aerobics instructors, or physical therapists, and move into managerial positions that involve more responsibility and earning potential. Those looking to break into a fitness career should be sure they have the appropriate knowledge and certifications before applying for positions. Health and fitness centers within gyms, resorts, corporate buildings, and cruise ships may advertise open positions in the newspaper or online at their Web sites. Professional associations, such as the Medical Fitness Association and the Aerobics and Fitness Association of America, have job boards that post openings in centers all over the country.

ADVANCEMENT

Because the job of fitness trainer is a higher-level management position, advancement is limited to moving to the same position within a larger fitness institution or becoming an owner of a fitness facility.

EARNINGS

Because many fitness directors start out in other positions, earnings can vary. Many individuals who eventually become directors major in exercise science. According to the American Society of Exercise

Physiologists, the salaries for those who have earned degrees in exercise science are as follows: bachelor's, $18,000 to $25,000; master's, $22,000 to $32,000; and doctorate, $30,000 to $60,000.

Once in a management position, fitness directors can earn much more, but their salaries still vary considerably depending on their experience and the size and location of their facility. Managers of personal service workers (the category under which the U.S. Department of Labor classifies fitness directors) earned median annual salaries of $32,800 in 2006. The lowest paid 10 percent earned less than $19,940, and the highest paid 10 percent earned $56,960 or more per year.

WORK ENVIRONMENT

With the pressure of balancing the needs of both clients and staff members, the job of fitness director can be demanding. However, the majority of directors work in comfortable workplaces. Most facilities maintain a cool temperature, are clean and well lit, and have well-cared-for equipment. Directors who work part time usually have to pay for their own benefits.

OUTLOOK

Opportunities within the fitness industry should grow much faster than the average for all occupations through 2014. In general, people are much more knowledgeable about exercise and nutrition. Businesses and medical professionals are promoting exercise as beneficial for both good health and increased work productivity. As the baby boomers grow older, they will increasingly rely on gyms, health clubs, and other fitness facilities to stay in shape. Knowledge of special weight training, stretching exercises, and diets for seniors will also drive older individuals to fitness institutions in the years to come.

FOR MORE INFORMATION

For a listing of jobs and certification information, contact
Aerobics and Fitness Association of America
15250 Ventura Boulevard, Suite 200
Sherman Oaks, CA 91403-3215
Tel: 877-968-7263
Email: contactAFAA@afaa.com
http://www.afaa.com

For general health and fitness topics, and to learn about certification, contact
American Council on Exercise
4851 Paramount Drive
San Diego, CA 92123-1449
Tel: 800-825-3636
Email: support@acefitness.org
http://www.acefitness.org

For information on certification, contact
American Fitness Professionals and Associates
PO Box 214
Ship Bottom, NJ 08008-0234
Tel: 800-494-7782
Email: afpa@afpafitness.com
http://www.afpafitness.com

For information on exercise physiology and certification, contact
American Society of Exercise Physiologists
c/o The College of St. Scholastica
1200 Kenwood Avenue
Duluth, MN 55811-4199
http://www.asep.org

For a listing of jobs in the fitness industry, contact
Medical Fitness Association
PO Box 73103
Richmond, VA 23235-8026
Tel: 804-897-5701
Email: info@medicalfitness.org
http://www.medicalfitness.org

Health Club Owners and Managers

QUICK FACTS

School Subjects
Business
English

Personal Skills
Communication/ideas
Leadership/management

Work Environment
Primarily indoors
Primarily one location

Minimum Education Level
Bachelor's degree

Salary Range
$19,940 to $32,800 to
$56,960+

Certification or Licensing
Recommended

Outlook
Much faster than the average

DOT
339

GOE
01.10.01, 11.01.01

NOC
0651

O*NET-SOC
39-1021.00, 39-9031.00

OVERVIEW

Health club owners and managers are responsible for the overall success of a fitness facility. Club owners buy, sell, and lease facilities, oversee top management, and play a role in the hiring and firing of staff. Club managers handle the daily operations of the club, such as hiring, training, and scheduling staff members, planning fitness programming, checking exercise equipment, and ensuring the safety and cleanliness of the club.

HISTORY

Medical professionals have long touted exercise as beneficial (if not necessary) to maintain health. In addition to a nutritional diet, daily exercise helps to maintain weight, aids circulation, and promotes lung and heart health. Many exercise by running, walking, biking, or skating in the great outdoors. However, for many people who live in harsh climates during much of the year, this is not always possible. There needs to be another option for those in Arizona in the middle of summer or those in Minnesota in the dead of winter. The introduction and rapid expansion of health clubs across the country fit this need.

According to an article by Phil Kaplan in *Muscle & Fitness* magazine, experts predict clubs will attract approximately 50 million members and will create 50,000 full-time and 150,000 part-time positions in the industry by 2010.

THE JOB

In general terms, health club managers, like other facility managers, coordinate the events that occur in the club with the services and people who make those events possible. This involves planning exercise programs, hiring trainers and class instructors, supervising facility redesign and construction, and overseeing the custodial staff who keep the club clean and safe. Depending on the size of the health club, managers may have different job titles and specialized duties, such as fitness directors (see the separate article on this career) or membership managers.

Health club owners are concerned with much more than the internal workings of the club. They must be sure they have the proper finances to keep the club running. This may require months, if not years, of research and long-term financial planning. Another crucial issue club owners must consider is how their club compares to others in the area. Does their club offer enough fitness options? Are the club's hours flexible for members with varying schedules? Is the cost of membership fair and competitive with other clubs? To determine these answers, owners may visit other health clubs to investigate their design, organization, and the types of classes offered.

Many health club owners expand their business beyond one location. To choose a new site, owners must analyze their finances and ensure that there is enough local support for a new club. Owners also must be aware of the area's zoning laws or other federal, state, and local regulations concerning the construction of new buildings.

In general, health club owners and managers spend most of their time in the office or somewhere within the health club itself, supervising the day-to-day management of the facility. Club owners determine the organizational structure of the facility and set personnel staffing requirements. As staffing needs arise, the club manager addresses them with the owner, who then sets the education, experience, and performance standards for each position. Depending on the size of the facility and the nature of managers' assigned responsibilities, hiring may be conducted by a separate personnel director or by the club's general manager.

REQUIREMENTS

High School

High school courses that will give you a general background for work in health club ownership or management include business, health, mathematics, physical education, and computer science.

Speech and writing classes will help you hone your communication skills. Managing a school club or other organization will give you an introduction to overseeing budgets and the work of others.

Postsecondary Training

A bachelor's degree is generally required to own or manage a heath club. Many owners and managers first work in lesser positions within the fitness industry to establish backgrounds in health or exercise science. The competition for jobs and increased complexity of owning and managing a facility (keeping the club in business and profitable) requires a strong background in business and finance. Many owners and managers hold a master's degree in business administration or sports facility management.

Certification or Licensing

Put simply, health clubs can bring owners a large amount of revenue, and these owners aren't willing to trust the management of such lucrative venues to individuals who are not qualified to run them. Certification is one way a health club owner can ensure that certain industry standards in club management are met. The International Facility Management Association, probably the industry leader in certification, offers the designations certified facility manager and facility management professional. The International Association of Assembly Managers also offers the certification designation of certified facilities executive. For contact information for these associations, see the end of this article.

Other Requirements

Most club owners require that higher-level managers have a minimum of five years of experience in the field or industry. This may include experience in other manager positions or in related fitness careers. Many managers end up in their management positions after first working as one of the club's staff members, such as an aerobics instructor or personal trainer.

In addition to experience, both owners and managers need to be strong communicators to work well with staff and relate well to the club's members. They need to be able to clearly and concisely state their ideas, information, and goals, regardless of their audience.

Health club owners, in particular, need to possess excellent strategic, budgetary, and operational planning skills to keep the club in business and to ensure profits. The owner's decisions affect all operations within the health club, so the owner needs to be capable of making the right choices and have the ability to juggle many different tasks.

EXPLORING

To be able to understand and meet the requirements of a health club career, you should be familiar with sports and fitness. Become involved in a sports team while in high school, as either a team member or a manager. Any experience helps, whether you're a star player, an equipment manager, or the team's statistician. You can also work with a local Booster Club to sponsor events that promote sports and fitness within your school district. These activities demonstrate your interest and devotion to sports and fitness and may help in the future by providing you with an edge when searching for a job.

Be sure to visit a health club, whether it is a small gym in your school or a large club in your neighborhood. While visiting, take some mental notes about the size and roles of the club's staff. Do you notice a manager on duty? How many pieces of exercise equipment are available? Is the club clean? If possible, ask a staff member about his or her job and how to get started in the industry. If you visit a local health club, ask if you can work out as a guest for a small fee. This will allow you to experience a club firsthand.

College students interested in sports facility management may be able to locate valuable internships through contacts they have developed from part-time jobs, but the placement centers in undergraduate or graduate programs in business administration and facility management are also good places to find information on internships.

EMPLOYERS

There are more than 14,000 commercial health clubs currently in operation. Fitness facilities may be chain operations or local establishments, or they may be owned by a larger corporation that offers the facility solely for the benefit of its employees.

STARTING OUT

Because of their growing popularity, clubs offer more part- and full-time positions than ever before. To find an employer near you, check for classified ads in local newspapers or online. You could also look up "health clubs" in a phone book and call or visit those in your area to ask about job opportunities.

Graduates of programs in sports administration and sports facility management usually find jobs through past internships, from personal contacts they developed in the field, or from job listings in their graduate programs' career services offices.

Many health club managers start out in other jobs. They may move into a management position after working in another fitness career. For example, an aerobics instructor who desires more management duties may become the club's fitness director. Other club managers are hired after first working in the business industry. For example, a public relations professional who is dedicated to working out may choose to leave his or her industry to work in health and fitness instead.

The job of health club owner is not a starting position. Most owners start out in other fitness industry positions, gaining the experience and financial know-how that are necessary for running a business.

ADVANCEMENT

Experience and certification are the best ways for someone to advance in a fitness career. Years of successful, on-the-job experience count for a great deal in this industry. Health club owners look for managers who have demonstrated the ability to run a club smoothly. Certification is another way in which success can be gauged. Since certification goes hand-in-hand with experience, it is assumed that those individuals who are certified are the best in their field.

Outside of experience and certification, a willingness and eagerness to learn and branch into new areas is another important factor affecting advancement. Those who are willing to embrace new technology and are open to new ideas and methods for improving the operation of their clubs will likely advance in their careers.

Health club managers who have strong business sense and financial backing may advance further by deciding to own their own clubs.

EARNINGS

Earnings for health club owners and managers depend on their experience and education, as well as the size of the facility. First-line supervisors/managers of personal service workers (the category under which the U.S. Department of Labor classifies health club owners and managers) earned median annual salaries of $32,800 in 2006. The lowest paid 10 percent earned less than $19,940, and the highest paid 10 percent earned $56,960 or more per year. Club managers who are certified earn higher salaries than those who are not certified. The International Facility Management Association reports that members who held the certified facility manager designation earn an average of $8,000 more than their noncertified counterparts.

WORK ENVIRONMENT

Health club owners and managers work in clean, comfortable surroundings. However, their jobs can be stressful and often require the ability to juggle many tasks at once. Managers and owners must constantly deal with the challenge of balancing the needs of staff members with the needs of the club's members—needs that may, at times, be at odds with each other.

Depending on the size of the club, the workload of owners and managers often requires that they work more than a standard eight-hour day. For managers, overtime is generally compensated by additional pay or time off. For owners, extra hours go unpaid; overtime simply comes with the territory of running a business.

OUTLOOK

The U.S. Department of Labor predicts much faster than average growth for the fitness industry through 2014. Because a growing number of people realize the importance of daily exercise for their general health and well-being, health clubs should continue to enjoy growth and popularity in the coming years. As the number of health clubs increases, so too will the demand for qualified individuals able to run them.

FOR MORE INFORMATION

For general health and fitness information, contact
American Council on Exercise
4851 Paramount Drive
San Diego, CA 92123-1449
Tel: 800-825-3636
Email: support@acefitness.org
http://www.acefitness.org

IDEA conducts surveys, provides continuing education, and publishes books and magazines relevant to the fitness industry. For more information, contact
IDEA Health & Fitness Association
10455 Pacific Center Court
San Diego, CA 92121-4339

Tel: 800-999-4332
Email: contact@ideafit.com
http://www.ideafit.com

For certification information, job listings, student chapters, and internships, contact
International Association of Assembly Managers
635 Fritz Drive, Suite 100
Coppell, TX 75019-4442
Tel: 972-906-7441
http://www.iaam.org

For information on certification, contact
International Facility Management Association
1 East Greenway Plaza, Suite 1100
Houston, TX 77046-0194
Tel: 713-623-4362
Email: ifma@ifma.org
http://www.ifma.org

To find the health club, fitness center, or gym nearest you, check out the following Web site
HealthClubDirectory.com
http://www.healthclubdirectory.com

Lifeguards and Swimming Instructors

OVERVIEW

Lifeguards and swimming instructors watch over and teach swimmers at public and private pools, beaches, health clubs, summer camps, private resorts, and public parks. Lifeguards enforce local laws and the particular regulations of their facility, and provide assistance to swimmers in need. One of their greatest responsibilities is preventing injuries and fatal accidents in or around water. Instructors hold group or individual swimming lessons. Most of their students are children, though instructors teach swimmers of all ages. Both lifeguards and instructors are trained professionals in the techniques of water rescue, cardiopulmonary resuscitation (CPR), and first aid.

HISTORY

Swimming was used first as a survival and hunting skill, and then became a popular sporting event. Early hieroglyphics in Egyptian tombs dating from 2500 to 2000 B.C. depict human figures swimming. Around 78 A.D., swimming was introduced and promoted in England, and by the 14th century, knights were required to be able to swim in their full body armor. The Olympics included swimming as a sport in 1896 for men and 1912 for women.

As swimming grew in popularity as a form of recreation, people frequented local beaches and swimming pools. Soon, there came a need for guards to patrol the waters and rescue swimmers in distress. There also came a need for certified instructors to teach

QUICK FACTS

School Subjects
Health
Physical education

Personal Skills
Helping/teaching
Leadership/management

Work Environment
Indoors and outdoors
Primarily one location

Minimum Education Level
High school diploma

Salary Range
$6.17/hour to $14.91/hour to $27.47/hour

Certification or Licensing
Required by all states

Outlook
About as fast as the average

DOT
379 (lifeguards)
153 (swimming instructors)

GOE
01.10.01

NOC
5254

O*NET-SOC
33-9092.00, 39-9031.00

new swimmers proper techniques to help them avoid emergencies in the first place.

The first lifeguards were loosely organized in groups similar to police or fire departments, and were often employees of the local government. However, training was not standardized—guards used a variety of lifesaving methods. The 1956 Summer Olympics in Australia spotlighted the profession with an exhibition/competition of international lifesavers. As a result, techniques, experience, and equipment such as the rescue tube, rescue buoy, and surfboard, were introduced to lifeguards worldwide. Today, lifeguards must meet strict standards of physical condition, professional training and skill. Many lifeguards use the *United States Lifesaving Association Manual of Open Water Lifesaving* as an important training guide.

Teaching techniques have also evolved over time. The dominating stroke for many years was the breaststroke, which was done with the head either in or out of the water, a side arm motion, and frog-like movement of the legs. Though this method of swimming was effective and thought to be graceful, it was not the fastest technique. In the mid 1950s, English amateur swimmer J. Arthur Trudgen took a trip to South America and noticed swimmers there with a different style. He brought the stroke back with him, calling it the Trudgen stroke, which, with changes from another competitive swimmer, Frederick Cavill, later became the still popular "crawl," or freestyle stroke. This technique, with arms moving up and over the head and legs kicking in a scissor-like motion, was soon used in competition and broke records of all distances. This freestyle stroke, along with the backstroke, the breaststroke, and the butterfly, are the main swimming techniques taught by instructors today.

THE JOB

Lifeguards patrol beaches, lakes, swimming pools, and other water areas, to ensure safety of the patrons and management of the facility. They monitor water activities to make sure all swimmers are safe. If swimmers go too far from shore or leave the designated swimming zone, the lifeguard is responsible for signaling the swimmer back to safer waters. In some cases, the lifeguard must physically bring the swimmer back. They also watch for any roughhousing in the water, as this may cause potential danger and injury. Lifeguards who are posted at lakes and ocean beaches must be on the watch for strong currents, changing weather conditions, and dangerous animals, such as jellyfish or sharks.

Lifeguards also enforce local laws or facility regulations. They must notify patrons if they are breaking beach rules such as drinking alcoholic beverages, using glass containers, swimming with pets,

A lifeguard zips up the safety vest of a toddler. *(Jeff Greenberg, The Image Works)*

or driving motorized vehicles. Swimming pools usually ban similar items; some pools also enforce certain time periods based on age.

Lifeguards keep watch from tower stations, or elevated chairs. The height is advantageous because it allows the lifeguard clear visibility of the facility, as well as keeping the station in the public's view. Whistles, megaphones, and binoculars are helpful tools for maintaining order. Lifeguards also use equipment, such as floatation devices, ropes, poles, and small boats, during rescue attempts. Lifeguards must be well versed in CPR and other first aid techniques—such knowledge may mean the difference between life and death with drowning victims. They not only need to be strong swimmers, but they must be levelheaded, calm, and ready to react in emergency situations.

Many lifeguards also work as swimming instructors. Instructors are hired by public pools, private swim clubs, and schools to teach proper swimming techniques. Generally teaching children or young adults, instructors show students how to swim using different strokes and breathing techniques. They also may teach students how to rescue or resuscitate swimmers during emergencies.

REQUIREMENTS

High School
Most facilities require their lifeguards and instructors to have a high school diploma, or a GED equivalent. High school classes in

physical education (especially swimming) and health will be helpful for this career.

Postsecondary Training

If you aspire to hold a pool or beach management position, such as pool manager or instructor supervisor or use your swimming training in a related career, then it would be wise to work toward a college degree. Consider degrees in health, recreation, or business.

Certification or Licensing

All lifeguards and instructors must be certified to work. Depending on their skill level, lifeguards must pass a training program, from basic lifeguard training to head lifeguard to aquatic professional. The basic lifeguard course lasts approximately six days and tests swimming skills. You will need to be able to swim 500 yards (no time frame) and tread water for one minute—as well as demonstrate your physical endurance, professionalism, and skills in using lifesaving equipment and techniques, CPR, and first aid. Head lifeguard courses teach advanced techniques in injury prevention, selection and training of guards, team building, and emergency response planning. To successfully complete the program, guards must attend and participate in the course, pass a written test, and demonstrate their guarding skills in the pool.

Instructors also must obtain certification to prove their teaching and swimming skills. The American Red Cross offers the designation water safety instructor to individuals 16 years of age or older. To earn this designation, candidates must attend and participate in the course, pass a written test, and prove their skills in techniques such as shallow and deep-water diving, rescue and lifesaving techniques, and demonstrate ability in all swimming strokes.

Other Requirements

Most training and certification programs require applicants to be at least 15 years of age. You should be in excellent physical condition, trustworthy, and able to exercise good judgment in serious situations. These jobs come with a tremendous amount of responsibility. Lifeguards are relied upon to keep water patrons safe and maintain order at their facility. Instructors are trusted with groups of small children who are not yet skilled at swimming.

EXPLORING

Do you want to test the waters *now?* If you are interested in lifeguarding, the United States Lifesaving Association offers junior lifeguard programs to students ages nine to 17. Participants learn water and beach safety and first aid techniques, as well as build self-confidence in the water.

Another way to explore these careers is by talking to lifeguards and instructors at your local pool or beach. Ask them how they got their jobs and learned swimming and guarding techniques. They may recommend certain programs for you to explore further. Finally, you can learn more about the work of lifeguards by reading *American Lifeguard Magazine* (http://www.usla.org/LGtoLG/mag.asp).

EMPLOYERS

Lakes and beaches are not the only work venues for lifeguards and swimming instructors. Hotels, schools, park districts, and health clubs all have swimming facilities, as well as public pools and institutions, such as the YMCA. Most places hire lifeguards and instructors on a temporary or seasonal basis. Opportunities for full-time employment are greater in areas that have warm weather year-round.

STARTING OUT

There is no standard way to enter this field. Many lifeguards and instructors find employment at facilities they normally frequent, or by word of mouth. The newspaper want ads are a good source—check under "Swimming Instructor," or "Lifeguard." Also, consider compiling a list of swimming facilities in your area and send job inquiries to those that interest you.

ADVANCEMENT

Many guards and instructors, employed on a temporary or seasonal basis, return to their jobs every summer until they finish school. There are quite a number of lifeguards and instructors who use their passion for the water and skills acquired while on the job as a basis for a full-time career. Dave Zielinski is a perfect example—he worked many summers as a lifeguard for his local YMCA. Today, he is employed as a customer service support manager for the Chicago chapter of the American Red Cross. Says Zielinski, "Lifeguarding gives an exciting avenue for those who enjoy the water."

There are other options as well. With hard work, ample experience, and further education, lifeguards and instructors can move into managerial positions such as *head lifeguard,* who assists managers and oversees all other guards; *aquatics manager,* who is responsible for the maintenance and operation of a pool; or *instructor supervisor,* who is involved in the hiring, training, and managing of all staff instructors. Highly skilled swimmers may choose to work as *aquatic specialists,* who run lifeguarding and instructor training programs or may even train professional swimmers.

EARNINGS

Earnings vary depending on several factors—facility or venue, hours worked, and certification status of the individual. Lifeguards had median hourly earnings of $8.25 (or $17,160 annually), according to the U.S. Department of Labor. Salaries ranged from less than $6.17 an hour (or $12,840 annually) to $12.23 an hour or more (or $25,440 annually).

According to the United States Lifesaving Association, those at the Lifeguard I level earned hourly wages that ranged from $9.54 to $18.75 in 2007. Lifeguard I is considered a seasonal or temporary appointment. Those at the Lifeguard II level earned wages that ranged from $14.91 to $27.47 in 2007. Lifeguard II is a permanent position.

Instructors may be paid per hour or per class. In general, they earn more for giving private lessons than teaching group sessions. According to a job posting on the summer employment Web site for the city of Salina, Kansas, instructor/lifeguards can earn between $6.50 and $7.50 per hour.

Full-time employees are often offered a benefits package consisting of paid vacation time, sick leave, health insurance, and a retirement plan.

WORK ENVIRONMENT

Employment in the sun, surf, and the outdoors may be the ideal work atmosphere for some. However, these jobs are anything but cushy. Lifeguards have a tremendous amount of responsibility when on duty. They must always be ready to prevent accidents and react quickly during emergencies, while resisting the distractions of the job environment. Similarly, instructors have to stay alert while teaching, especially when instructing young children. Instructors also have the added stress of teaching young students who may not enjoy their time in the pool, and as a result, may not cooperate or be on their best behavior.

Though instructors teach classes of varying lengths, most lifeguards work eight-hour shifts. Depending on the size of the facility, guards work in pairs or teams. "Expect long hours in the sun," says Dave Zielinski—especially if you are stationed outdoors.

OUTLOOK

The outlook for lifeguards and instructors is mixed. Public interest in health and physical fitness is increasing steadily. Also, water amusement parks, a collection of swimming pools, wave pools and water slides, are gaining in popularity. Combined with lakes, beaches, private and public swimming pools, not to mention pools located within high schools and universities, the opportunity for employment is plentiful. However, most lifeguard and instructor positions are part time, or seasonal, mainly during the summer months. There are some swimming facilities open year-round, though these jobs are rare. Many students take lifeguard or instructor positions to supplement their income until they finish school. Those who desire to have a full-time career as a lifeguard or instructor should seek the best training available, and consider a college education, as well as advanced training in swimming and lifesaving procedures and techniques.

FOR MORE INFORMATION

For information regarding certification, education, or class schedules, contact
American Red Cross
2025 E Street, NW
Washington, DC 20006-5009
Tel: 202-303-4498
http://www.redcross.org

For information on careers and the junior lifeguard program, contact
United States Lifesaving Association
Tel: 866-FOR-USLA
http://www.usla.org

Motivational Speakers

QUICK FACTS

School Subjects
English
Speech

Personal Skills
Communication/ideas
Helping/teaching

Work Environment
Primarily indoors
Primarily multiple locations

Minimum Education Level
High school diploma

Salary Range
$100/speech to $1,000/
speech to $2,500/speech

Certification or Licensing
Recommended

Outlook
About as fast as the average

DOT
N/A

GOE
N/A

NOC
N/A

O*NET-SOC
N/A

OVERVIEW

Motivational speakers give inspirational and informative speeches to groups of people. They are hired by businesses, schools, resorts, and communities to speak on topics such as achieving personal or financial success, living a healthy lifestyle, or organizing one's personal life or business. Speakers must tailor their message to their audience, whether it is a class of high school students or a group of business executives.

HISTORY

Motivation is the internal drive that urges people to act in a certain way. People are motivated through the expectation of a reward, whether tangible (such as a cash bonus) or intangible (such as internal satisfaction). People can also be motivated by fear of the loss of privileges or power (such as employment termination).

Throughout history, people have been motivated by different factors. During tough economic periods, people are motivated by money or even food. In good times, people are still motivated by money, but they can also find motivation in achieving intangible things such as success or publicity.

Though motivational speaking may seem like a recent invention, speakers have long been influencing people. Even Jesus Christ can be considered a motivational speaker. Political leaders such as Abraham Lincoln and Martin Luther King Jr. have motivated people to act in a certain way.

A more recent development is the hiring of motivational speakers to inspire smaller and more specific audiences. Whether motivational speakers are addressing a group of professional baseball players about improving their performance on the field, or talking to a graduating class of college students about making it in the real world, their ultimate goal is the same: to motivate.

THE JOB

Motivational speakers are hired to speak on a variety of topics, depending on their audience and specialty. They may talk about overcoming alcohol or drug abuse, achieving athletic success, developing business skills, coping with change, communicating with others, working with computers, welcoming diversity, dealing with gender issues, protecting self-esteem, negotiating with a boss, improving performance, handling relationships, adjusting to retirement/aging, or managing stress—to name a few. Many speakers talk about how they overcame an obstacle and how others can do the same. They speak to young students, single parents, business professionals, school administrators, or any other group looking for advice and motivation.

Speakers need to worry about more than just delivering their speech. They have to prepare for the talk weeks or even months in advance, rehearsing their delivery and pinpointing their message to their specific audience.

On the day of their speech, motivational speakers should arrive at the location of their speech early to make sure that everything is in place. Some speakers like to use microphones, while others are able to project their voice without using one. Some motivational speakers like to walk around while speaking and may require a cordless microphone, while others are more comfortable standing at a podium. All these details have to be worked out in advance to make sure the speech goes smoothly.

Speaking in public is something many people dislike, even fear, doing. But motivational speakers have to speak in front of audiences large and small on a regular basis. They have to sound confident, knowledgeable, and compassionate with their listeners. They must make any performance fears that they have work for them—adding energy to their speech instead of nervousness.

Most importantly, motivational speakers must be engaging. Speakers shouldn't speak to their audience; they should speak with them. Everyone has faced hardships in life. For this reason, motivational speakers must try to relate to their audience members' experiences on some level. While speaking about overcoming obstacles such as depression, drug abuse, or joblessness, speakers may use funny, touching, or shocking stories from their own lives to connect with their listeners.

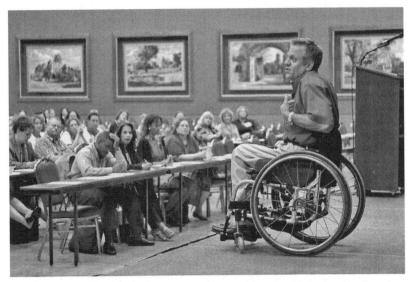

Retired Paralympic tennis player and now motivational speaker Randy Snow talks about overcoming adversity at an association convention. (Bob Daemmrich, The Image Works)

REQUIREMENTS

High School

Motivational speakers should have a high school diploma at the very least. Obvious class choices should include English and speech, but drama, foreign language, and computer classes would also be useful. Depending on what topic you wish to speak on, you could also take classes in business, history, science, or math—practically any area about which you feel passionately.

Postsecondary Training

A communications degree, though not required, would be useful for a job in public speaking. Advanced classes in speech, writing, and English will help you hone your communication skills and make you a stronger, more confident speaker. Again, depending on your specialty, you could also major in business, finance, political science, or other subject areas, but be sure to take communications classes on the side.

Certification or Licensing

To increase their credibility and marketing appeal, many motivational speakers seek certification to demonstrate their skills and experience. The National Speakers Association offers the certified speaking professional (CSP) designation to professional speakers with many years of experience earning money from speeches. Applicants must meet high standards, including meeting certain educational requirements, having five years of public speaking experience, giving a certain number of presentations to audiences of 15 or more, working with a specified number of different clients, earning a minimum gross speaking income, and mastering a variety of professional competencies grouped under the following areas: expertise, eloquence, enterprise, and ethics. The association also gives the title CSP candidate to individuals who have met some of these standards and are working toward full certification.

Other Requirements

Motivational speakers must be very confident in order to be able to speak in front of an audience. Besides being good communicators, speakers need to be able to connect with their listeners on a personal level. They should be compassionate and understanding and maintain a positive outlook on life. To be able to motivate and inspire others, they must be motivated and inspiring themselves! For their stories to be believable, speakers have to be honest about their experiences and not be afraid to share sometimes vulnerable moments in order to get their messages across.

EXPLORING

To get a sense of what this career is like, you should take advantage of public speaking opportunities while in school. Participate in school plays to gain experience and skills performing in front of an audience. If your school has a speech or debate team, join and work on your speaking and debate skills. You will have to prepare your own argument and deliver it in front of people, including judges that are evaluating your delivery, use of eye contact, and overall performance.

Read magazines such as *Speaker* to learn about hot topics and developments within the profession. Sample articles are available on the National Speakers Association's Web site at http://www. nsaspeaker.org.

EMPLOYERS

Motivational speakers are hired by a variety of clients. Depending on the focus of their speeches, they are hired by schools, government agencies, small businesses, large corporations, resorts, health clubs, spas, and even cruise lines.

Most are self-employed and work for clients on a one-time basis. Some speakers have repeat clients, such as speakers who are hired to give a presentation at an annual conference. Speakers who focus on employee training may be hired full time to train new workers directly or teach managers about training methods.

STARTING OUT

It is difficult to work full time as a motivational speaker. Most speakers work part time until they develop a list of clients and build a solid reputation as a speaker. To start out, many speakers offer to talk for free or for a nominal fee. This will give them experience and references for future clients.

Most speakers prepare promotional packets to send out to potential clients. These include an introductory letter, a resume, references, a color photo, and a "demo" videotape or DVD of one of their speeches.

Clients also may choose to join a professional organization such as the American Speakers Bureau Corporation for exposure and job assistance. Speakers are listed on the organization's Web site, http://www.speakersbureau.com, by specialty and region.

ADVANCEMENT

Motivational speakers advance by working for larger clients, earning more money per speech, or working full time. Popular motivational speakers can advance by working more in the spotlight, hosting radio or television programs, writing books, or running Web sites. A good example of this type of personality is Dr. Phil McGraw, personal growth specialist, speaker, writer, and TV host.

EARNINGS

According to Mike Moore, motivational speaker and operator of a Web site, Speak for Profit (http://www.speakforprofit.com), beginning speakers can expect to earn between $100 and $200 per speech, in addition to reimbursement for any expenses incurred. Within a year, dedicated and talented speakers can earn $400 to $1,000 per speech, $1,500 to $2,000 for a longer seminar, and $2,000 to $2,500 for a full day of speaking. A National Speakers Association survey reported that 26.6 percent of its members earned fees between $3,001 and $5,000 per presentation in 2005. Of those surveyed, 18.7 percent earned fees of $1,000 or less per presentation, with 2.8 percent earning less than $100 per presentation. At the other end of the salary scale, 3 percent also reported earning more than $10,000 per presentation.

It is important to note that earnings can be sporadic and depend wholly on the ability of the speaker to find clients and appointments.

WORK ENVIRONMENT

Motivational speakers work in a variety of locations, from business boardrooms to school cafeterias. They generally speak indoors but may work outdoors on occasion, such as during a graduation ceremony.

When not "talking," speakers generally work from home, gathering information for their next assignment and looking for new business opportunities.

While giving speeches, motivational speakers work in what many may consider a stressful environment, with hundreds and maybe thousands of people watching and listening. But to the successful motivational speaker, this environment is viewed as thrilling and captivating.

OUTLOOK

Membership in the National Speakers Association has increased by 30 percent in the last decade, indicating growth in the speaking profession. However, the job market for motivational speakers depends on their specialty and targeted audiences. Those who speak at schools are affected by budget cuts that can make the hiring of professional speakers a financial impossibility. Those who speak to professional associations, however, are seeing growth in the number of job opportunities available. According to a recent study by the American Society of Association Executives, nearly half of all seminars and three-fourths of all conventions hosted by associations include a professional speaker as part of their scheduling.

Because of the nature of the job, motivational speakers will always find opportunities to impart their wisdom. However, like other self-employed workers, it's the speaker's resourcefulness and marketability that will determine his or her success.

FOR MORE INFORMATION

To learn more about this professional association of speakers, contact

American Speakers Bureau Corporation
10151 University Boulevard, #197
Orlando, FL 32817-1904
Tel: 407-826-4248

Email: info@speakersbureau.com
http://www.speakersbureau.com

For information about certification and training programs, contact
National Speakers Association
1500 South Priest Drive
Tempe, AZ 85281-6203
Tel: 480-968-2552
http://www.nsaspeaker.org

For information on membership and other resources for speakers in Canada, contact
Canadian Association of Professional Speakers
1370 Don Mills Road, Suite 300
Toronto, ON M3B 3N7 Canada
Tel: 416-847-3355
Email: info@canadianspeakers.org
http://www.canadianspeakers.org

Personal Trainers

OVERVIEW

Personal trainers, often known as *fitness trainers*, assist health-conscious people with exercise, weight training, weight loss, diet and nutrition, and medical rehabilitation. During one training session, or over a period of several sessions, trainers teach their clients how to achieve their health and fitness goals. They train in the homes of their clients, their own studio spaces, or in health clubs. More than 65,000 personal trainers work in the United States, either independently or on the staff of a fitness center.

HISTORY

For much of the second half of the 20th century, "98-pound weaklings" were tempted by the Charles Atlas comic book ads to buy his workout plan and to bulk up. Atlas capitalized on a concern for good health that developed into the fitness industry after World War II. Though physical fitness has always been important to the human body, things have changed quite a bit since the days when people had to chase and hunt their own food. Before the Industrial Revolution, people were much more active, and the need for supplemental exercise was unnecessary. But the last century has brought easier living, laziness, and processed snack foods.

Even as early as the late 1800s, people became concerned about their health and weight and began to flock to spas and exercise camps. This proved to be a passing fad for the most part, but medical and nutritional studies began to carefully explore the significance of exercise. During World War II, rehabilitation medicine proved more effective than extended rest in returning soldiers to the front line.

QUICK FACTS

School Subjects
Health
Physical education

Personal Skills
Communication/ideas
Helping/teaching

Work Environment
Primarily indoors
Primarily multiple locations

Minimum Education Level
Some postsecondary training

Salary Range
$14,880 to $25,910 to $71,080+

Certification or Licensing
Recommended

Outlook
Much faster than the average

DOT
153

GOE
01.10.01

NOC
5254

O*NET-SOC
39-9031.00

Even the early days of TV featured many morning segments devoted to exercise. The videotape revolution of the 1980s went hand in hand with a new fitness craze, as Jane Fonda's workout tapes became best-sellers and inspired a whole industry of fitness tapes and books. Now most health clubs offer the services of personal trainers to attend to the health and fitness concerns of its members.

THE JOB

Remember the first time you ever went to the gym? The weight machines may have resembled medieval forms of torture. So, to avoid the weight training, you stuck to the treadmill. Or maybe you called upon the services of a personal trainer. Personal trainers help their clients achieve health and fitness goals. They instruct on the proper use of exercise equipment and weight machines and may suggest diet and nutrition tips.

If you've reached your own workout goals, then you may be ready to help others reach theirs. "You have to believe in working out and eating healthy," advises Emelina Edwards, a personal trainer in New Orleans. For 12 years she's been in the business of personal training, a career she chose after whipping herself into great shape at the age of 46. Now, at 58, she has a lot of first-hand experience in training, nutrition, aerobic exercise, and stress management. Edwards says, "You have to practice what you preach."

And practice Edwards does—not only does she devote time every day to her own weight training, jogging, and meditation, but she works with three to five clients in the workout facility in her home. She has a total of about 20 clients, some of whom she assists in one-on-one sessions, and others in small groups. Her clients have included men and women from the ages of 20 to 80 who are looking to improve their general physical condition or to work on specific ailments.

When meeting with a client for the first time, Edwards gets a quick history of his or her physical problems and medical conditions. "If problems are serious," Edwards says, "I check with their doctor. If mild, I explain to them what I believe will help." When she discovered that four out of five people seeking her help suffered from back problems, she did a great deal of research on back pain and how to alleviate it through exercise. "I teach people how to do for themselves," she says. "Sometimes I see a person once, or for three or four sessions, or forever."

In addition to working directly with clients, Edwards is active promoting her line of "Total Body Rejuvenation" products. These products, consisting of audiotapes and books, are based on her years

A personal trainer supervises a woman during a workout. *(Jeff Greenberg, The Image Works)*

of experience and the many articles she has written for fitness publications. When she's not training clients, writing articles, and selling products, she's reading fitness publications to keep up on the business, as well as speaking at public events. "When I realized I loved training," she says, "I thought of all the things I could relate to it. So along with the training, I began to write about it, and to give talks on health and fitness."

Successful personal trainers do not necessarily have to keep as busy as Edwards. They may choose to specialize in certain areas of personal training. They may work as an *athletic trainer*, helping athletes prepare for sports activities. They may specialize in helping with the rehabilitation treatment of people with injuries and other physical problems. Yoga, dance, martial arts, indoor cycling, boxing, and water fitness have all become aspects of special training programs. People call upon personal trainers to help them quit smoking, to assist with healthy pregnancies, and to maintain mental and emotional stability. Whatever the problem, whether mental or physical, people are turning to exercise and nutrition to help them deal with it.

Many personal trainers have their own studios or home gyms where they train their clients; others go into the homes of their clients. Because of the demands of the workplace, many personal trainers also work in offices and corporate fitness centers. Though most health clubs hire their own trainers to assist with club members, some hire freelance trainers as independent contractors. These independent contractors are not considered staff members and do not receive employee benefits. (IDEA Health and Fitness Association found that 30 percent of the personal trainers hired by the fitness centers surveyed were independent contractors.)

REQUIREMENTS

High School

If you are interested in health and fitness, you are probably already taking physical education classes and involved in sports activities. It is also important to take health courses and courses like home economics, which include lessons in diet and nutrition. Business courses can help you prepare for the management aspect of running your own personal training service. Science courses such as biology, chemistry, and physiology are important for your understanding of muscle groups, food and drug reactions, and other concerns of exercise science. If you are not interested in playing on sports teams, you may be able to volunteer as an assistant. These positions will allow you to learn about athletic training as well as rehabilitation treatments.

Postsecondary Training

A college education is not required to work as a personal trainer, but you can benefit from one of the many fitness-related programs offered at colleges across the country. Some relevant college programs include health education, exercise and sports science, kinesiology, fitness program management, and athletic training. These programs include courses in therapeutic exercise, nutrition, aerobics, and fitness and aging. IDEA recommends a bachelor's degree from a program that includes at least a semester each in anatomy, kinesiology, and exercise physiology. IDEA offers scholarships to students seeking careers as fitness professionals.

If you are not interested in a full four-year program, many schools offer shorter versions of their bachelor's programs. Upon completing a shorter program, you'll receive either an associate's degree or certification from the school. Once you have established yourself in the business, continuing education courses are important for you to keep up with the advances in the industry. IDEA is one of many organizations that offer independent study courses, conferences, and seminars.

Certification or Licensing

There are so many schools and organizations that offer certification to personal trainers that it has become a concern in the industry. Without more rigid standards, the profession could suffer at the hands of less experienced, less skilled trainers. Some organizations only require membership fees and short tests for certification.

The U.S. Department of Labor reports that personal trainers must be certified in the fitness field to find employment, and health clubs look for certified trainers when hiring independent contractors. If you are seeking certification, you should choose a certifying board that offers scientifically based exams and requires continuing education credits. The American Council on Exercise, the National Federation of Professional Trainers, and American Fitness Professionals and Associates are just a few of the many groups with certification programs.

Other Requirements

Physical fitness and knowledge of health and nutrition are the most important assets of personal trainers. "The more intelligently you can speak to someone," Edwards says, "the more receptive they'll be." Your clients will also be more receptive to patience and friendliness. "I'm very enthusiastic and positive," she says regarding the way she works with her clients. You should be able to explain things clearly, recognize progress, and encourage it. You should be comfortable working one-on-one with people of all ages and in all physical conditions. An interest in reading fitness books and publications is important to your continuing education.

EXPLORING

Your high school may have a weight-training program, or some other extracurricular fitness program, as part of its athletic department; in addition to signing up for the program, you can assist the faculty who manage it. That way, you can learn about what goes into developing and maintaining such a program. If your school doesn't have a fitness program, seek one out at a community center, or join a health club.

You should also try the services of a personal trainer. By conditioning yourself and eating a healthy diet, you'll get a good sense of the duties of a personal trainer. Any number of books and magazines address issues of health and nutrition and offer weight-training advice. The IDEA publishes several helpful health- and career-related publications including *IDEA Fitness Journal* and *IDEA Trainer Success*.

Finally, seek out part-time work at a gym or health club to meet trainers and learn about weight machines and certification programs.

EMPLOYERS

IDEA reports that there are more than 65,000 personal trainers working in the United States. Personal trainers are employed by people of all ages. Individuals hire the services of trainers, as do companies for the benefit of their employees. Though most health clubs hire personal trainers full time, some clubs hire trainers on an independent contractor basis. Sports and exercise programs at community colleges hire trainers part time to conduct classes.

Personal trainers can find clients in most major cities in all regions of the country. In addition to health clubs and corporate fitness centers, trainers find work at YMCAs, aerobics studios, and hospital fitness centers.

STARTING OUT

Most people who begin personal training do so after successful experiences with their own training. Once they've developed a good exercise regimen and healthy diet plan for themselves, they may feel ready to help others. Emelina Edwards had hit a low point in her life, and had turned to weight training to help her get through the difficult times. "I didn't have a college degree," she says, "and I needed something to do. All I had was weight training." She then called up all the women she knew, promoting her services as a personal trainer. Through the benefit of word-of-mouth, Edwards built up a clientele.

Some trainers begin by working part time or full time for health clubs and, after making connections, they go into business for themselves. As with most small businesses, personal trainers must promote themselves through classified ads, flyers posted in community centers, and other forms of advertisement. Many personal trainers have published guides on how to establish businesses.

ADVANCEMENT

After personal trainers have taken on as many individual clients as they need to maintain a business, they may choose to lead small group training sessions or conduct large aerobics classes. Some trainers join forces with other trainers to start their own fitness centers. Trainers employed by fitness centers may be promoted to the position of *personal training director*. These workers supervise and schedule other personal trainers and manage department budgets.

Emelina Edwards has advanced her business by venturing out into other areas of fitness instruction, such as publishing books and speaking to groups. "I want to develop more in the public speaking arena," she says. Right now, she only speaks to local groups—she'd like to go national. "I'd also like to break into the Latin market," she says. "The interest is there, and the response has been great."

EARNINGS

The IDEA reports that the average hourly rate for personal trainers is $41. Hourly fees ranged from less than $20 to $70 or more. Personal trainers who offer specialized instruction (such as in yoga, martial arts, or indoor cycling), or who work with their own clients in their own homes, can charge higher hourly rates. The U.S. Department of Labor reports that in 2006 the median annual salary for fitness trainers, which includes personal trainers, was $25,910. The lowest paid 10 percent earned $14,880 or less and the highest paid 10 percent earned $56,750 or more. A 2007 Salary.com survey found that salaries for personal trainers ranged from less than $24,505 to $71,080 or more.

WORK ENVIRONMENT

Personal training is obviously a physically demanding job, but anybody who is in good shape and who eats a healthy diet should be able to easily handle the demands. Personal trainers who work out of their homes will enjoy familiar and comfortable surroundings. Trainers who work in a gym as independent contractors will also experience a comfortable workplace. Most good gyms maintain a cool temperature, keep the facilities clean and well-lit, and care for the weight machines. Whether in a gym or at home, personal trainers work directly with their clients, usually in one-on-one training sessions. In this teaching situation, the workplace is usually quiet and conducive to learning.

As with most self-employment, sustaining a business can be both rewarding and difficult. Many trainers appreciate being able to keep their own hours, and to work as little, or as much, as they care to. By setting their own schedules, they can arrange time for their personal workout routines. But, without an employer, there's less security, no benefits, and no steady paycheck. Personal trainers have to regularly promote their services and be ready to take on new clients.

OUTLOOK

Fitness training will continue to enjoy strong growth in the near future. The U.S. Department of Labor predicts employment opportunities for personal trainers and other fitness workers to grow much faster than the average for all occupations through 2014. As the baby boomers grow older, they will increasingly rely on the services of personal trainers. Boomers have long been interested in health and fitness, and they will carry this into their old age. A knowledge of special weight training, stretching exercises, and diets for seniors will be necessary for personal trainers in the years to come. Trainers will actively promote their services to senior centers and retirement communities.

With the number of health publications and fitness centers, people are much more knowledgeable about exercise and nutrition. This could increase business for personal trainers as people better understand the necessity of proper training and seek out professional assistance. Trainers may also be going into more of their clients homes as people set up their own workout stations complete with weights and treadmills. In the health and medical field, new developments are constantly affecting how people eat and exercise. Personal trainers must keep up with these advances, as well as any new trends in fitness and dieting.

FOR MORE INFORMATION

For information on certification, contact
American College of Sports Medicine
PO Box 1440
Indianapolis, IN 46206-1440
Tel: 317-637-9200
http://www.acsm.org

For general health and fitness topics, and to learn about certification, contact
American Council on Exercise
4851 Paramount Drive
San Diego, CA 92123-1449
Tel: 800-825-3636
Email: support@acefitness.org
http://www.acefitness.org

For information on certification, contact
American Fitness Professionals and Associates
PO Box 214
Ship Bottom, NJ 08008-0234
Tel: 800-494-7782
Email: afpa@afpafitness.com
http://www.afpafitness.com

IDEA conducts surveys, provides continuing education, and publishes books and magazines relevant to personal trainers. For information about the fitness industry in general, and personal training specifically, contact
IDEA Health and Fitness Association
10455 Pacific Center Court
San Diego, CA 92121-4339
Tel: 800-999-4332
Email: contact@ideeafit.com
http://www.ideafit.com

For information on certification, contact
National Federation of Professional Trainers
PO Box 4579
Lafayette, IN 47903-4579
Tel: 800-729-6378
http://www.nfpt.com

INTERVIEW

Kelleen Kenny is a personal trainer in Orland Park, Illinois. She discussed her career with the editors of Careers in Focus: Coaches and Fitness Professionals.

Q. How long have you worked in the field? Please tell us about yourself and your business.

A. I have been working in the fitness industry since 2003. I first became certified as a group fitness instructor and followed with personal training. I began training clients in their homes two-and-a-half years ago. Currently, I am a personal trainer at a health club where I also teach group fitness classes. I also work as a preschool teacher and created a fitness class for four, five, and six year olds called "Fitness and More." We talk about nutrition, health, and fitness as a part of their everyday lives and learn how to make healthy choices. The children also exercise and learn about different muscle groups. I teach about six adult exercise classes a week and have approximately five to seven clients, two to three times a week.

Q. What made you want to enter this career?

A. I always wanted to be a gym teacher. I love the idea of working out as a part of my life and to be able to teach this idea is so rewarding. I truly love to see clients transform over a period of time with healthy long-term benefits. It is such a pleasure to work one on one with people, giving them the attention they need to reach their goal.

Q. Please briefly describe your primary and secondary job responsibilities.

A. My primary job is to help the client reach particular goals. Each and every client is different; that's why we call it "personal training." I find out what the client's goals are and work at helping them reach them. I also like to educate the client by keeping them informed of health, nutrition, and fitness news, as the field seems to change [regularly]. The client needs to know that the personal trainer's job is just a small equation of their lives, and they need to continue their goals even when they are on their own. Health and fitness IS a part of *every day* life!

Q. What are some of the pros and cons of your job?

A. Becoming a personal trainer can be a great career choice because you can make your own days and hours. You can decide if you want to work out of your home, go to the home of a client, or work at a club or gym. Sometimes, it can be difficult when you need to work around other people's schedules, especially when you have many clients. Many people work 9-5, which will have you working into the evening hours. Also, you may have clients that prefer to train prior to work, which may mean early morning appointments. Once you establish which is best for you and your client, you may have hours throughout the day and night. All in all, it can be a very flexible and rewarding job.

Depending on where you live most personal trainers make a decent salary—anywhere from $25 to $100 an hour.

Most reputable outfits require that you attend workshops and conferences to remain certified as a trainer. It is a requirement to earn a certain amount of continuing education units a year. This can be costly but it does ensure that trainers stay updated and knowledgeable about new and upcoming products, equipment, health, nutrition, etc.

Q. What activities would you suggest to high school students who are interested in this career?

A. Any high school student who is interested in a fitness career should join a gym. Learning how to properly use equipment is helpful and beneficial. Also, I find that becoming a counselor or a coach at a younger age teaches leadership. Taking exercise classes, participating in running clubs, or even joining the track team or sports teams at school or with the township will also help provide exercise adherence.

Q. What advice would you give to young people who are interested in becoming personal trainers?

A. Personal training is a good job choice if you like to work with the public. It also is a very physical job. I think it is very important to go to college and look into fitness certifications. Most offer a 30-hour credit course that consists of about 10 different classes including anatomy, kinesiology, fitness programming, leadership, etc. On the other hand, weekend certifications are also available. These consist of just a two-day study class with practical and written tests. If you choose this route, I recommend at least six months of study before taking the test.

Physical Education Teachers

OVERVIEW

Physical education (PE) teachers instruct students in kindergarten through grade 12 about physical fitness and health. They may organize physical education programs for an entire school or just a few classes. PE teachers make up only a small percentage of the approximately 3.8 million teachers employed in the United States.

HISTORY

In the United States, organized physical education is less than 200 years old. In 1823, George Bancroft, a historian and statesman, opened the Round Hill School in Northampton, Massachusetts. In 1825, Bancroft hired Charles Beck to teach Latin and physical education. Beck, a follower of Friedrich Ludwig Jahn, a German known as the "Father of Gymnastics," is often considered to be the first physical education teacher in the United States. Amherst College (Massachusetts) opened the first department of physical education in the United States in 1860. One year later, the physician Dioclesian Lewis founded the Normal Institute of Physical Education in Boston, Massachusetts. It was the first school to prepare teachers of physical education. Following the Civil War, physical education became part of many educational programs.

In the early 20th century, physical education programs expanded and improved rapidly. Between 1901 and 1925, 32 states passed physical education legislation requiring some sort of physical training in schools.

By the early 1950s, fitness tests revealed that American children were lagging behind their European counterparts. In response, President Eisenhower formed the Council on Youth Fitness, which eventually became the President's Council on Physical Fitness and Sports. Physical fitness programs grew in popularity in schools. They focused largely on activities that developed athletic skills, such as calisthenics and competitive sports.

During the past two decades, physical education classes have been under attack by school systems interested in saving money and improving academic performance in traditional academic disciplines. The introduction of classes such as computer science, art, foreign language, and music into school curriculums has also reduced the time allotted for physical education classes.

According to the National Association for Sport and Physical Education, only about half of K–12 students and only 29 percent of high school students have physical education classes daily. In 2005, only 25 percent of all students attended a PE class, according to the Centers for Disease Control and Prevention (CDC)—down from 42 percent of students in 1991. Illinois is the only state in the nation that requires daily PE, but, since 1995, Illinois schools have been allowed to seek waivers to exempt them from compliance.

These reductions in physical education programs have contributed to an increasing epidemic of overweight and obese children. Today, 9 million children and teens ages six to 19 are overweight—a 300 percent increase since 1980, according to the U.S. Department of Health and Human Services. The CDC reports that the number of obese children has nearly tripled in the past 20 years to one in three. Health problems for overweight and obese children include heart disease, high cholesterol, high blood pressure, and the development of type 2 diabetes (a disease previously limited to adults).

Ironically, studies have shown clear links between athletic fitness and academic success. A 2001 study by the California Department of Education found a strong relationship between academic achievement and the physical fitness of students in its public schools. Reading and mathematics scores were matched with the fitness scores of nearly one million fifth-, seventh-, and ninth-grade students. The fittest students had higher academic achievement levels, especially in mathematics.

Physical education classes today focus on the development of fitness skills, nonathletic competition, individual exercise goals, and aerobic training. This new approach to physical education is often referred to as "the new PE." Madison Junior High School in Naperville, Illinois, is an excellent model of how the new PE is changing the lives of young people. While kids at Madison still participate in team sports during gym class, PE instructors also teach them how to use exercise bikes, weights, inline skates, and treadmills. The school even has a rock-climbing wall that students can use. According to an article on the Web site CNNStudentNews, Madison students are graded on how well they stay within heart-rate zones rather than who runs the fastest. Students also receive a computer printout that records their heart rate, body fat, and cholesterol levels. Students are tracked through the 12th grade. Approximately 30 percent of schools in Illinois have changed to this new physical education model.

Public officials are beginning to see the value of physical education in the schools. Congress passed The Physical Education for Progress Act in 2000. It authorizes the Secretary of Education to award grants to school districts to start, expand, and improve K–12 physical education programs. Grants may be used to purchase athletic equipment, develop curriculum, and hire and train physical education staff.

As a result of this legislation and continuing lobbying efforts by physical education advocacy organizations, PE teachers can expect an optimistic employment outlook for their field.

THE JOB

Physical education teachers, through participation in individual and team sports, lectures, and other activities, educate students about fitness, nutrition, and general health. They use their knowledge of sports techniques and human physiology to develop exercise plans for students at the kindergarten through high school levels. Physical education programs not only develop the physical abilities of students but also help them to develop personal attributes such as self-discipline, sportsmanship, judgment, communication skills, teamwork, self-confidence, self-esteem, and the ability to set and meet goals. PE teachers may work alone or with one or more PE teachers and may be employed at more than one school.

According to the Council of Physical Education for Children, physical education teachers use different methods of instruction based on the age of their students. *Elementary school physical education teachers* use educational games, basic dance, gymnastics, and other activities to help their students develop important motor skills such as throwing, jumping, skipping, hopping, kicking, and catching. Instructors at this level usually teach eight to 10, 30-minute classes daily.

Middle school students require a more systematic and structured approach to physical education. *Middle school physical education teachers* use traditional sports (such as volleyball and basketball), adventure activities (such as rock climbing, rope climbing, and skiing), and leisure activities (such as inline skating and biking) to help students stay fit. They set performance goals and assess the fitness levels of their students. Middle school PE instructors teach three to six classes daily. These classes last from 60 to 90 minutes.

High school students are much more physically, emotionally, and intellectually developed than elementary and middle school students. They are more likely to choose sports activities based on their own interests, and they take more responsibility for health and fitness choices. While continuing to educate students about traditional, adventure, and leisure activities, *high school physical education teachers* focus on helping students establish positive habits and attitudes about exercise and fitness. They help students explore and develop their specific sports and fitness interests with the hope that they will continue to remain fitness- and health-conscious during the rest of their lives. High school PE instructors teach three to six classes daily. These classes last from 60 to 90 minutes.

After each class, physical education teachers store equipment that was used during class. They order supplies and new equipment. They might also write up notes on how students performed during the class.

Outside of the gym or fitness center, physical education teachers prepare lesson plans and activities. They evaluate student work and calculate grades. In the process of planning their classes, PE teachers read fitness and health-related magazines, books, and Web sites to learn more about their field. They practice exercises or fitness activities in order to be able to better demonstrate them to students. They also continue to study alternative and traditional teaching methods to hone their skills. PE teachers attend educational conferences to learn more about their field. They attend faculty meetings, parent-teacher conferences, and state and national teacher conferences. Many PE teachers have the opportunity for extracurricular work as athletic coaches. They also monitor students during lunch, break times, and study halls. They may accompany student groups on field trips and to competitions and events. High school PE teachers may be required to teach health classes as part of their duties.

Some physical education teachers are trained to teach those with disabilities. Special physical education is a federally mandated part of special education services. *Adapted physical education teachers* modify, adapt, and/or change a physical activity so that it can be done by students who have disabilities. Disabilities include mental retardation, orthopedic impairment, speech or language impairment, attention deficit hyperactivity disorder, autism, behavioral disorders, cerebral palsy, visual impairments, hearing impairments, and learning disabilities.

REQUIREMENTS

High School
In addition to taking physical education and participating in as many sports as possible, take college preparatory classes, including mathematics, science, and psychology. You should also take speech and English courses to develop your communication skills.

Postsecondary Training
You will need to earn a minimum of a bachelor's degree in health and physical education to work as a physical education teacher. Typical classes for this major include exercise physiology, kinesiology, health and wellness, first aid/cardiopulmonary resuscitation (CPR), sports psychology, teaching physical education/health, and activity courses that teach the fundamentals of specific sports such as golf, aerobics, basketball, tennis, and track.

An advanced degree is usually required to teach physical education at the college level. Visit http://www.gradschools.com for a list of schools that offer graduate programs in sports and physical education.

There are more than 500 accredited teacher education programs in the United States. Most of these programs are designed to meet the certificate requirements for the state in which they are located. Some states may require that you pass a test before being admitted to an educational program. You may choose to major in your subject area while taking required education courses, or you may major in secondary education with a concentration in your subject area. You will probably have advisors (both in education and in your chosen specialty) to help you select courses.

In addition to a degree, a training period of student teaching in an actual physical education environment is usually required. Students are placed in schools to work with full-time teachers. During this period, undergraduate students observe the ways in which lessons are presented and the gym or fitness center is managed. Students also learn how to keep records of such details as attendance and grades and get actual experience in handling the class, both under supervision and alone.

Certification or Licensing
Voluntary teacher certification in physical education is available from the National Board for Professional Teaching Standards (NBPTS).

Applicants must have a bachelor's degree and three years of classroom experience in a public or private school. They must prepare a portfolio of their teaching experience and complete exercises at an NBPTS assessment center to demonstrate their knowledge of their teaching specialty. After they complete these requirements and pay an application fee, they can use the designation, national board certified teacher (NBCT). Certifications are available in early and middle childhood and early adolescence through young adulthood. Certification is valid for 10 years and is renewable. For more information, visit http://www.nbpts.org/standards/nbcert.cfm.

The American Board for Certification of Teacher Excellence also offers voluntary certification. Prospective teachers can earn the passport to teaching certification and experienced teachers can earn the master teacher certification. Visit http://www.abcte.org for more information.

The National Consortium on Physical Education and Recreation for Individuals with Disabilities offers a voluntary certification program for adapted physical education instructors. Instructors who pass an exam and meet other professional requirements may use the professional designation, certified adapted physical educator (CAPE). For more information on this certification, visit http://www.cortland.edu/apens.

Public school teachers must be licensed under regulations established by the department of education of the state in which they teach. Not all states require licensure for teachers in private or parochial schools. When you have received your teaching degree, you may request that a transcript of your college record be sent to the licensure section of your state department of education. If you have met licensure requirements, you will receive a certificate and thus be eligible to teach in the public schools of your state. In some states, you may have to take additional tests. If you move to another state, you will have to resubmit college transcripts, as well as comply with any other regulations in the new state, to be able to teach there.

Other Requirements

To be a successful PE teacher, you must be in good physical shape. You must have knowledge of human physiology and the psychological factors involved in physical education. You must also be willing to continue to learn about physical education and fitness and like helping children learn fitness techniques and maintain good overall health. You need strong interpersonal and instructional skills to be able to communicate well with students. You should also be well organized, as you will have to keep track of the work and progress of many students.

Adolescence can be a troubling time for children, and these troubles often affect behavior and performance. This will require you to be very patient because children learn at different levels. You must also have good motivational skills to be able to properly motivate students who do not want to participate in class or perform up to appropriate levels. Because you will be working with students who are at very impressionable ages, you should serve as a good role model.

EXPLORING

Consider ordering a student subscription to periodicals such as the *Journal of Teaching in Physical Education* and the *Journal of Physical Activity and Health*. These publications, popular with PE teachers, will give you a useful overview of the field. Both of these publications can be ordered at the Human Kinetics Web site, http://www.humankinetics.com.

Becoming a student member of the American Alliance for Health, Physical Education, Recreation & Dance will allow you to access information on health and physical education as well as receive the periodicals *Strategies: A Journal for Physical and Sport Educators* and the *Journal of Physical Education, Recreation & Dance*. For more information, visit http://www.aahperd.org.

By attending gym class, you've already gained a good sense of the daily work of a physical education teacher. But the requirements of a teacher go far beyond the gym or fitness center, so ask your PE teachers if you can talk with them after school. Interview your teachers about the amount of work that goes into preparing a class and directing activities. Look into coaching an athletic team, counseling at a summer camp, or working part time at a fitness center. This will give you experience coaching and interacting with young people.

EMPLOYERS

Physical education instructors are employed at public and private schools. They work in elementary schools, middle schools, junior high schools, high schools, junior colleges, and four-year universities. They are also employed by boys/girls clubs, camps, health spas and resorts, correctional facilities, martial arts studios, dance studios, resorts, community centers, child care facilities, fitness centers, health clubs, and gyms.

STARTING OUT

After completing your student teaching and becoming certified, you will work with your college's career services office to find a

On the Web

Fitness.com
http://fitness.com

Fitness
http://www.fitnessmagazine.com

The Fitness Jumpsite
http://primusweb.com/fitnesspartner

Get Active Stay Active!
http://www.getactivestayactive.com

Library of Sport, Coaching and Physical Education
http://www.pedigest.com

PE Central
http://www.pecentral.org

PE4life
http://pe4life.org

PE Program Web Sites
http://www.pecentral.org/websites/peprogramsites.html

President's Council on Physical Fitness and Sports
http://www.fitness.gov and http://www.presidentschallenge.org

Shape Up America
http://www.shapeup.org

full-time position. The departments of education of some states maintain listings of job openings. Many schools advertise teaching positions in the classified sections of major newspapers. You may also directly contact the principals and superintendents of the schools in which you would like to work. While looking for full-time work, you can work as a substitute teacher. In urban areas with many schools, you may be able to substitute full time. PE Central, an organization for health and physical educators, also offers job listings for physical education teachers at its Web site, http://www.pecentral.org.

Once you get called for an interview, it is important that you make a good impression on the interviewer. Visit PE Central's Web site for a list of interview tips and sample interview questions for prospective PE teachers.

ADVANCEMENT

Most physical education teachers advance simply by becoming more of an expert in the field. They usually receive an increase in salary as they acquire experience. Additional training or study can also bring an increase in salary.

A few PE teachers who have management ability and an interest in administrative work may advance to the position of principal. Others may advance into supervisory positions or teach aspiring physical educators at colleges and universities. For most of these advanced positions, additional education is required. Some PE teachers also make lateral moves into other education-related positions such as guidance counselor.

Physical education instructors may choose to advance by working outside of the physical education field. With further education and experience, PE instructors can become exercise physiologists, sports trainers, sports nutritionists, fitness industry workers, coaches, and kinesiologists.

EARNINGS

The National Association of Colleges and Employers reports that the average starting offer for new graduates with a bachelor's degree in education, which includes physical education teaching/coaching was $31,015 in 2005.

The U.S. Department of Labor reports that the median annual salary for elementary school teachers was $45,570 in 2006. The lowest paid 10 percent earned less than $30,370; the highest paid 10 percent earned $72,720 or more. Middle school teachers earned salaries that ranged from less than $31,450 to $73,350 or more in 2006. Secondary school teachers had median earnings of $47,740 in 2006. Ten percent earned less than $31,760, and 10 percent earned $76,100 or more annually. Recreation and fitness studies teachers at the postsecondary level earned median salaries of $49,270 in 2006.

In general, teachers who obtain certification receive higher salaries than teachers who are not certified.

Most teachers are contracted to work nine months out of the year, though some contracts are made for 10 months or a full year. In most cases, teachers have the option of prorating their salary up to 52 weeks. Teachers can also supplement their earnings through teaching summer classes, coaching sports, sponsoring a club, or other extracurricular work.

On behalf of teachers, unions bargain with schools over contract conditions such as wages, hours, and benefits. A majority of teachers join the American Federation of Teachers or the National Education Association. Depending on the state, teachers usually receive a retirement plan, sick leave, and health and life insurance. Some systems grant teachers sabbatical leave.

WORK ENVIRONMENT

Physical education teachers work in generally pleasant conditions. Some older schools may have poor heating and cooling systems. Instructors teach some classes outdoors in hot, cold, rainy, and other challenging weather conditions. School hours are generally 8:00 A.M. to 3:00 P.M., but all teachers work more than 40 hours a week teaching, preparing for classes, assessing grades, and directing extracurricular activities. As a coach or faculty adviser for an extracurricular activity, physical education instructors may have to work some evenings and weekends.

This job can be occasionally tiring and trying. Physical education instructors are on their feet for many hours each day explaining and demonstrating fitness activities. They must also handle disciplinary problems, which take them away from teaching students. Physical education instructors teach classes that are as small as 20 or fewer students or as large as 100 to 200 students. Some PE teachers may have to teach excessively large classes due to budget cuts and understaffing. This can lead to stress and burnout.

Students, parents, and school administrators may approach physical education with skepticism and a lack of respect. They may feel that PE is not as important an academic discipline as geometry, chemistry, or foreign language. PE teachers must be willing to educate these people regarding the benefits of proper fitness for children and discuss how modern physical education programs build life skills and reduce serious health problems in children.

Some physical education teachers who are employed at more than one school may have to travel back and forth between schools during their workdays.

OUTLOOK

Physical fitness is growing in popularity in the United States. The President's Council on Physical Fitness and Sports continues to encourage children and adults to be fit. A majority of adults and teens surveyed in 2003 by the National Association for Sport and Physical Education feel that physical education should be mandatory in schools. Although physical education programs continue to be cut, there is hope that this renewed interest in exercise and fitness will reverse this trend. The U.S. Department of Education predicts average growth for preschool, elementary, middle, and secondary school teachers through 2014.

FOR MORE INFORMATION

For information on student membership, contact
American Alliance for Health, Physical Education, Recreation and Dance
1900 Association Drive
Reston, VA 20191-1598
Tel: 800-213-7193
Email: info@aahperd.org
http://www.aahperd.org

For information on teacher certification, contact
American Board for Certification of Teacher Excellence
1225 19th Street, NW, Suite 400
Washington, DC 20036-2457
Tel: 877-669-2228
http://www.abcte.org

For information about union membership, contact the following organizations
American Federation of Teachers
555 New Jersey Avenue, NW
Washington, DC 20001-2029
Tel: 202-879-4400
http://www.aft.org

National Education Association
1201 16th Street, NW
Washington, DC 20036-3290
Tel: 202-833-4000
http://www.nea.org

For information on health issues for students and physical education teachers, contact
American School Health Association
7263 State Route 43
PO Box 708

Kent, OH 44240-0013
Tel: 330-678-1601
Email: asha@ashaweb.org
http://www.ashaweb.org

For information on professional membership, contact
National Association for Sport and Physical Education
1900 Association Drive
Reston, VA 20191-1598
Tel: 703-476-3400
Email: naspe@aahperd.org
http://www.aahperd.org/naspe

For information on teacher certification, contact
National Board for Professional Teaching Standards
1525 Wilson Boulevard, Suite 500
Arlington, VA 22209-2451
Tel: 800-228-3224
http://www.nbpts.org/nbct

For information on the CAPE designation, contact
National Consortium on Physical Education and Recreation for
    Individuals with Disabilities
Tel: 607-753-4969
Email: apens@cortland.edu
http://www.cortland.edu/apens

*For information on accredited teacher education programs and
teaching careers, contact*
National Council for Accreditation of Teacher Education
2010 Massachusetts Avenue, NW, Suite 500
Washington, DC 20036-1023
Tel: 202-466-7496
http://www.ncate.org

For comprehensive resources for health and physical educators, visit
PE CENTRAL
http://www.pecentral.org

*PE4life is an advocacy group that promotes more and better physi-
cal education in schools. For more information, contact*
PE4life
http://pe4life.org

INTERVIEW

David Martinez is an adapted physical educator in Cherokee County, Georgia. He teaches students with disabilities in elementary, middle, and high schools. Additionally, he provides consultative services to general physical educators who include students with disabilities in their classes, and was recently accepted as the Georgia State Adapted Physical Education National Standards Coordinator. David discussed his career with the editors of Careers in Focus: Coaches and Fitness Professionals.

Q. How long have you worked as an adapted physical educator?

A. I began teaching adapted physical education for the Pasco County School District (Florida) in 1995–1996. I moved to North Georgia in 1998 and was employed by the Cherokee County School District (CCSD). During my first year with the CCSD, I taught general physical education and advocated for an adapted physical education program. In 1999 the school district hired me and another physical educator to create an adapted physical education program. The program was created to meet the unique educational needs of students with severe disabilities in our county. Additionally, we were hired to act as consultants to general physical educators who serve students with disabilities. The program continues to grow. Currently, the program consists of three full-time adapted physical educators.

Q. Please describe a day in your life on the job.

A. My teaching responsibilities include providing direct services to children with moderate to severe and profound disabilities. Sometimes, I co-teach with general physical educators. Other times, I collaboratively work with physical, occupational, and speech therapists. In some of my self-contained physical education classes, non-disabled peers join in and participate alongside their peers with disabilities. This model facilitates equal-status relationships and allows all of my students and peer helpers to appreciate individual differences.

Another important job responsibility is consulting with general physical educators. Most physical educators teach students with disabilities. I assist with lesson planning and activity modifications to meet the educational needs of the students. Our goal is to provide developmentally and functionally appropriate activities for all students.

Additionally, I have to do formal evaluations on students. This evaluation process assists us in deciding the most appropriate placement for students with disabilities. Furthermore, evaluation results are used to create annual goals and short-term objectives to be included in the student's Individualized Education Program. I also co-coordinate the Cherokee County Special Olympics program.

Q. How did you train for this job? What was your college major?

A. I attended the University of South Florida in Tampa. The university had an outstanding adapted physical education teacher preparation program under the direction of Dr. Louis Bowers. While enrolled at the university, I was awarded a grant funded by the U.S. Office of Special Education. This grant enabled me to earn a graduate degree with an emphasis in adapted physical education. Recently, I was certified by the National Consortium on Physical Education and Recreation for Individuals with Disabilities as a nationally certified adapted physical educator. For certification, candidates must sit for an exam and demonstrate expertise in the 15 Adapted Physical Education National Standards.

Q. What are the most important personal and professional qualities for adapted physical educators?

A. The most important quality for an adapted physical educator to possess is the capability to appreciate and accommodate the unique ability levels of the students they teach. This attribute requires creativity and patience. Adapted physical educators oftentimes work in multiple school sites. Being able to adjust to the unique school site procedures is necessary. Additionally, it is vital to have outstanding interpersonal skills. Most adapted physical educators establish close working relationships with multidisciplinary teams consisting of administrators, classroom teachers, general physical educators, therapists, school psychologists, behavior specialists, and parents. Professionally, it is crucial for the adapted physical educator to demonstrate competency in the Adapted Physical Education National Standards.

Q. What are some of the pros and cons of your job?

A. The most rewarding part of my job is when I encourage and witness my students successfully participating in meaningful and functional physical activities in the school gymnasium as well as the community. Taking time to volunteer and coach athletes with disabilities is a wonderful and life-enriching experience. Recently, one of the teams I coach won the gold medal in the Georgia State Special Olympics Games. Those experiences are so motivating and give me a tremendous amount of occupational pride.

The most difficult part of my job is scheduling. It can be difficult to schedule instruction time around the students' classroom instruction and therapy sessions. Being an itinerant can also be difficult, especially during rainy days. I travel to more than 10 schools a week with little planning time. As a result, my car doubles as my office and equipment room.

Q. What is the future employment outlook for adapted physical educators?

A. Public Law 108-466 (The Individuals with Disabilities Education Act, or IDEA) states that physical education is a required service to students who qualify for special education services. Furthermore, physical education is specifically defined in the IDEA's definition of special education. Due to this legislation, school boards are encouraged to hire nationally certified adapted physical educators to provide quality programming to students with disabilities.

Professional Sports Coaches

OVERVIEW

Professional sports coaches instruct and manage professional athletes. These athletes compete in individual-player sports such as tennis, figure skating, golf, track and field, and boxing, or as members of baseball, football, basketball, hockey, soccer, and other sports teams. Coaches prepare their players for competition. During competition, coaches oversee their players and use their knowledge of the sport to try to beat the opposing player or team. Over 90,000 elementary, secondary, postsecondary, and professional sports coaches are employed in the United States. Professional coaches comprise a very small percentage of this group.

HISTORY

Prior to the 19th century, most sports were not officially organized; there were no official rules, competitions, or standards of play. During the 19th century, however, many sports shifted from invented pastime to official sport. Rules governing play, the field of play, and the nature of competitions were developed. The first modern track-and-field meet, for example, was held in England in 1825. Meanwhile, in the United States, the English game of rugby evolved into American football. The first game was played between Rutgers University and Princeton University in 1869. Baseball was invented in 1839, and the first professional league was formed in 1876. The game of basketball was invented in 1891 by James Naismith, a young physical education teacher in Springfield, Massachusetts.

QUICK FACTS

School Subjects
Physical education
Speech

Personal Skills
Communication/ideas
Helping/teaching
Leadership/management

Work Environment
Indoors and outdoors
Primarily multiple locations

Minimum Education Level
Some postsecondary training

Salary Range
$13,990 to $26,950 to
$8,000,000+

Certification or Licensing
None available

Outlook
About as fast as the average

DOT
153

GOE
01.10.01

NOC
5252

O*NET-SOC
27-2022.00

Baseball, basketball, golf, tennis, and boxing began to attract large crowds of people in the early 20th century. As these sports and others grew in popularity, governing bodies and organizations were created to oversee the fair play of each sport. Gradually, coverage of sporting events in newspapers and on the radio began to grow until sports quite literally became the national pastime for Americans. As sports grew in popularity and professional leagues were formed for all the major sports, professional coaches were increasingly relied on to manage and teach players.

Today, professional sports are still growing in popularity, and professional coaches enjoy considerable prestige and high salaries. Coaches may not be as popular as star athletes, but they still play a very important role in sports competition.

THE JOB

Many professional teams have several coaches per team. *Head coaches* are the top coaches of a sports team. They are assisted by *assistant coaches,* who specialize in one aspect of the sport. In professional baseball, for example, the head coach, known as a *manager,* oversees a group of coaches with specialized skills. These assistant coaches include a *bench coach,* who assists the manager in game situations; a *pitching coach,* who works with the team's starting and relief pitchers; a *hitting* or *batting coach,* who works with the team's hitters; a *bull-pen coach,* who is responsible for making sure that pitchers warm up correctly before they enter a game; *first* and *third base coaches,* who advise players on base-running after they reach base; and *strength and conditioning coaches,* who help players maintain top performance levels. Some Major League Baseball teams may even have a coach who teaches players proper base-running techniques.

Coaches oversee practices and workouts to help athletes develop fundamental skills and condition their bodies for competition. They use lectures and demonstrations to instruct their players on the proper way to play their sports. Professional sports coaches are experts in the rules and strategies for their respective sports. They use this expertise to make decisions during games. Coaches are also responsible for maintaining team discipline. Professional athletes occasionally behave poorly on and off the field. Coaches must address these behavioral problems or other issues that may affect the team's performance. Coaches must be consistent and fair when assessing penalties for misbehavior; otherwise they will lose the confidence of their team.

Professional athletes are the top athletes in their sports. It is assumed, but not always true, that they are experts at every aspect of their sport, from blocking and running offensive routes in football to fielding a ground ball and bunting in baseball. If a player is deficient in an area, a sports coach may work with the player to improve his or her abilities or assign an assistant coach to help the player.

Most coaches will tell you that psychological preparation is every bit as important as physical training in professional-level sports. One of the most important and challenging jobs for a professional coach is the motivation of star athletes who sometimes do not give maximum effort during competition. It is the coach's job to motivate athletes to give their best effort in every game as well as make sacrifices for the benefit of the team. Players require different motivation methods based on their personalities. Some players respond well to criticism, while others may respond better to positive reinforcement. Coaches must know what psychological approach to use with each player.

All professional sports leagues have a preseason when teams compete in exhibition games. Sports coaches use this exhibition season to teach players fundamental skills, help players regain top levels of conditioning lost during the off-season, and evaluate new and current players to determine if they have the ability to be part of the team. By the end of the preseason, the coach must choose a final group of players that will make up the team. The remaining players are released (the equivalent of being fired from a traditional job) or sent to the minor or lower level leagues for more training and experience. Sports coaches must explain to these players why they did not make the team and give them encouragement and tips on how to eventually make it to the professional level.

To prepare for competition, coaches develop game plans based on the skills and talents of their athletes and the strengths and weaknesses of the opposing team or athlete. They go over these game plans with their players, covering any scenarios that may occur during competition. In team sports such as basketball, soccer, and baseball, coaches choose a starting lineup and have a general idea of which players they will substitute into the game. Game action also affects how a coach uses his or her players. For example, an injury to a player early in a game might force the coach to alter his or her game plan.

During competition, professional coaches analyze their team's play and revise their strategy if necessary. They substitute players into the game if a starting player gets tired, is injured, or is not performing up to his or her abilities. They also substitute players for strategic reasons. (In the team sport of baseball, a player cannot reenter the game after he is removed by the manager. For this reason, baseball managers need strong organizational skills to keep track of which players have been used and which players are still available for competition.) Coaches need to keep track of timeouts, playing time remaining in the game, the number of fouls each player has received, and other issues.

On off days, coaches review film of recent games to assess the performances of their players. They take notes on the tendencies and actions of the opposing team's players to plan for future contests between the teams. Coaches meet with assistant coaches to discuss player issues or develop strategy for upcoming games.

Coaches work with general managers and other top management to assess players. They offer advice on which players the team should

A baseball coach (left) for the Baltimore Orioles offers instruction to a player during spring training. *(Jon Way, Reuters, Corbis)*

acquire through amateur drafts or through trades or free agent signings. Sports coaches also work with sports nutritionists, team physicians, sports trainers, sports psychologists, exercise psychologists, sports scouts, and marketing and public relations specialists.

Sports coaches also have administrative responsibilities. They attend league meetings with owners, assistant coaches, and general managers, who oversee the day-to-day operations of the team. Coaches hire and fire assistant coaches. If a coaching vacancy occurs, coaches interview candidates and choose a replacement. In some sports, the general manager may be responsible for hiring and firing coaches.

Coaches meet with newspaper, radio, and television reporters before and after games to discuss their players and the decisions they made during a game. Coaches also speak at charity events, awards dinners, and fan fests, and on radio and television talk shows.

REQUIREMENTS
High School
To prepare for a coaching career, you should take physical education, human physiology, biology, psychology, and health classes. Courses in English and speech will help you to communicate effectively with your players, assistant coaches, and team management. Participation in high school sports will give you useful exposure to competition, rules and regulations, and game situations—skills you will need as a coach.

Postsecondary Training
A college degree is not required to become a professional sports coach, but many coaches often attended college as athletes. Since no one begins their coaching career at the professional level, it is vital that you earn a college degree so that you will have a firm educational background as you work your way up the coaching ladder. Many coaches earn degrees in business, recreation, education, sports management, or other subject areas in which they have an interest. Aspiring coaches often begin their coaching careers at the high school and college levels. Most high school and college coaches work as teachers in addition to their coaching duties. To become a teacher, you will need at least a bachelor's degree in education, physical education, or another area of interest.

Other Requirements
To be a successful professional coach, you must have an encyclopedic knowledge of the sport that you coach. You also need to have considerable playing and coaching experience. You should be a

good communicator in order to instruct and interact successfully with your players and assistant coaches, team management, and the media. You also need to be disciplined and have the patience to accept mistakes and losses. Coaches must also be able to work in high-pressure situations and be able to accept criticism from fans and media during losing streaks.

You will also need to stay up to date with new coaching techniques and rule procedures, have a desire to continue to learn, and be willing to try new strategies and techniques.

EXPLORING

Begin coaching and playing sports as early as possible. Get involved in school or community leagues in a variety of sports. Attend sporting events as a spectator. Observe how the head coach manages and interacts with players, and think about what you would do in various game situations. If you are a member of a team, talk with your sports coach about his or her career, or ask your school guidance counselor to set up an informational interview with a sports coach in your community.

EMPLOYERS

Professional sports coaches are employed by private and public ownership groups all over the world. At the highest professional level for male athletes, there are 32 National Football League franchises, 30 Major League Baseball franchises, 30 National Basketball Association franchises, 30 National Hockey League franchises, and 13 Major League Soccer franchises in the United States and Canada. The Women's National Basketball Association has 13 franchises in the United States. Most professional sports leagues also have minor leagues that employ sports coaches. Professional sports coaches who coach individual players in tennis, figure skating, and other individual sports are usually self-employed. Professional coaches make up only a very small percentage of the more than 90,000 sports coaches employed in the United States.

STARTING OUT

Professional sports coaching is not an entry-level career. Almost every professional sports coach played and coached for many years in high school, college, or the minor leagues before being hired at the professional level. Once you establish a proven track record as a coach, you will be able to pursue more lucrative and challenging coaching positions at higher professional levels.

If you are interested in coaching at the college level, you might try to land a job as a *graduate assistant coach*. Graduate assistant coaches are recently graduated players who are interested in becoming coaches. You will receive a small stipend and, more importantly, gain valuable coaching experience.

ADVANCEMENT

Professional sports coaches advance based on their individual skills and coaching abilities. Assistant coaches can advance to fill head coaching positions with their team or another team. Some head coaches advance to the position of general manager. Occasionally, a top coach may work as both head coach and general manager. Coaches of individual-player sports advance by coaching athletes who consistently win competitions. This allows them to ask for higher salaries and be more selective regarding clients and work schedules.

EARNINGS

Salaries for professional sports coaches vary widely depending on the sport, the person or team being coached, and the skill level of the coach. The coach of a Masters champion, for example, commands a higher salary than the coach of a professional golf player who has never won a tournament. The coach of a Super Bowl champion earns a lot more than a rookie coach who has no proven track record in the National Football League.

The U.S. Department of Labor reports that the median earnings for sports coaches at all levels of competition were $26,950 in 2006. The lowest paid 10 percent earned less than $13,990, while the highest paid 10 percent earned more than $58,890.

Coaches for professional teams often earn between $200,000 and $3 million. Some top coaches command even higher salaries. The highest paid coaches in the National Basketball Association earn between $6 million and $7 million annually. Top coaches in Major League Baseball earn between $2 million and $7.5 million annually, while the highest paid National Football League coaches earn about $8 million a year. Professional sports coaches usually receive two- to five-year contracts based on their past experience as head or assistant coaches on winning teams. Many popular coaches augment their salaries with income from personal appearances and endorsements.

WORK ENVIRONMENT

The work environment for professional sports coaches varies by sport. Many professional sports competitions such as football, baseball, soccer, and track are held both indoors and outdoors. Other sports, such as basketball and hockey, take place only indoors. Indoor competitions are held in climate-controlled stadiums. Outdoor competitions take place in a variety of weather conditions depending on the sport. For example, a professional football team may play one game in wintry conditions in Wisconsin and their next game in warm and sunny Florida.

Professional sports teams compete all over the world. They play exhibition or real games in other countries. Professional coaches and athletes usually travel by plane, but occasionally they travel to nearby cities by bus or train. They usually stay in first-class hotels when traveling.

Coaches often work 16 hours each day, five or six days a week during their playing season. They often spend their off days analyzing game film or making public appearances. Many games are held on nights and weekends because this is when fans are able to watch teams play. This busy schedule can be tough on a coach's personal life.

There is little job security in professional sports coaching. Professional sports is big business, and sports media, fans, and team owners expect professional sports coaches to produce winning teams. When their teams don't perform up to expectations, coaches are often fired or reassigned. Coaches can be fired at any time, but they still receive their salaries if they are under contract.

OUTLOOK

Professional sports leagues employ relatively few coaches, and competition for existing jobs is very strong. The creation of new professional leagues, as well as the expansion of current leagues, will open some new employment opportunities for professional coaches. Other openings will arise as coaches retire or are terminated. Coaching is an exciting, demanding profession, but there is little job security in this field.

FOR MORE INFORMATION

For general information on sports and fitness, contact
American Alliance for Health, Physical Education, Recreation and Dance
1900 Association Drive
Reston, VA 20191-1598

Tel: 800-213-7193
Email: info@aahperd.org
http://www.aahperd.org

For information on careers in sports and physical education, contact
National Association for Sport and Physical Education
1900 Association Drive
Reston, VA 20191-1598
Tel: 800-213-7193
Email: naspe@aahperd.org
http://www.aahperd.org/naspe

Visit the following Web sites for more information on professional sports:
Association of Tennis Professionals
http://www.atptennis.com

Ladies Professional Golf Association
http://www.lpga.com

Major League Baseball
http://www.mlb.com

Major League Soccer
http://www.mlsnet.com

National Basketball Association
http://www.nba.com

National Football League
http://nfl.com

National Hockey League
http://www.nhl.com

Professional Golf Association
http://www.pga.com

Women's National Basketball Association
http://www.wnba.com

Women's Tennis Association
http://www.wtatour.com

Recreational Therapists

OVERVIEW

Recreational therapists plan, organize, direct, and monitor medically approved recreation programs for patients in hospitals, clinics, and various community settings. These therapists use recreational activities to assist patients with mental, physical, or emotional disabilities to achieve the maximum possible functional independence. Recreational therapists hold approximately 24,000 jobs in the United States.

HISTORY

The field of therapy has expanded in the past few decades to include recreational therapy as a form of medical treatment. Its use grew out of the realization that soldiers suffering from battle fatigue, shock, and emotional trauma respond positively to organized recreation and activity programs.

As a result, therapy for people in nursing homes, hospitals, mental institutions, and adult care facilities is no longer limited to physical therapy. Experiments have shown that recovery is aided by recreational activities such as sports, music, art, gardening, dance, drama, field trips, and other pastimes. Elderly people are more healthy and alert when their days are filled with activities, field trips, and social get-togethers. People with disabilities can gain greater self-confidence and awareness of their own abilities when they get involved with sports, crafts, and other activities. People recovering from drug or alcohol addiction can reaffirm their self-worth through directed hobbies, clubs, and sports. The recreational therapist is a health professional who organizes these types of activities and helps patients take an active role in their own recovery.

THE JOB

Recreational therapists work with people who are mentally, physically, or emotionally disabled. They are professionals who employ leisure activities as a form of treatment, much as other health practitioners use surgery, drugs, nutrition, exercise, or psychotherapy. Recreational therapists strive to minimize patients' symptoms, restore function, and improve their physical, mental, and emotional well-being. Enhancing the patient's ability to take part in everyday life is the primary goal of recreational therapy; interesting and rewarding activities are the means for working toward that goal.

Recreational therapists work in a number of different settings, including mental hospitals, psychiatric day hospitals, community mental health centers, nursing homes, adult day care programs, residential facilities for those with mental disabilities, school systems, and prisons. They can work as individual staff members, as independent consultants, or as part of a larger therapeutic team. They may get personally involved with patients or direct the work of assistants and support staff.

The recreational therapist first confers with the doctors, psychiatrists, social workers, physical therapists, and other professionals on staff to coordinate their efforts in treatment. The recreational therapist needs to understand the nature of the patient's ailment, current physical and mental capacities, emotional state, and prospects for recovery. The patient's family and friends are also consulted to find out the patient's interests and hobbies. With this information, the recreational therapist then plans an agenda of activities for that person.

To enrich the lives of people in hospitals and other institutions, recreational therapists use imagination and skill in organizing beneficial activities. Sports, games, arts and crafts, movie screenings, field trips, hobby clubs, and dramatics are only a few examples of activities that can enrich the lives of patients. Some therapists specialize in certain areas. *Dance/movement therapists* plan and conduct dance and body movement exercises to improve patients' physical and mental well-being. *Art therapists* work with patients in various art methods, such as drawing, painting, and ceramics, as part of their therapeutic and recovery programs. Therapists may also work with pets and other animals, such as horses. *Music therapists* design programs for patients that can involve solo or group singing, playing in bands, rhythmic and other creative activities, listening to music, or attending concerts. Even flowers and gardening can prove beneficial to patients, as is proved by the work of *horticultural therapists*. When the treatment team feels that regular employment would help certain patients, the *industrial therapist* arranges a productive job for the patient in an actual work environment, one that will have the greatest therapeutic value based on the patient's needs and abilities. *Orientation therapists* for the blind work with people who have recently lost their sight, helping them to readjust to daily living and independence through training and exercise. All of these professional therapists plan their programs to meet the needs and capabilities of patients. They also carefully monitor and record each patient's progress and report it to the other members of the medical team.

As part of their jobs, recreational therapists need to understand their patients and set goals for their progress accordingly. A patient having trouble socializing, for example, may have an interest in playing chess but be overwhelmed by the prospect of actually playing, since that involves interaction with another person. A therapist would proceed slowly, first letting the patient observe a number of games and then assigning a therapeutic assistant to serve as a chess partner for weeks or even months, as long as it takes for the patient to gain enough confidence to seek out other patients for chess partners. The therapist makes a note of the patient's response, modifies the therapy program accordingly, and lets other professionals know of the results. If a patient responds more enthusiastically to the program, works more cooperatively with others, or becomes more disruptive, the therapist must note these reactions and periodically reevaluate the patient's activity program.

Responsibilities and elements of the job can vary, depending on the setting in which the recreational therapist works. In nursing homes, the therapist often groups residents according to common or shared interests and ability levels and then plans field trips, parties, entertainment, and other group activities. The therapist documents residents' responses to the activities and continually searches for ways of heightening residents' enjoyment of recreational and leisure activities, not just in the facility but in the surrounding community as well. Because nursing home residents are likely to remain in the facility for months or even years, the activities program makes a big difference in the quality of their lives. Without the stimulation of interesting events to look forward to and participate in, the daily routine of a nursing home can become monotonous and depressing, and some residents are apt to deteriorate both mentally and physically. In some nursing homes, recreational therapists direct the activities program. In others, activities coordinators plan and carry out the program under the part-time supervision of a consultant who is either a recreational or occupational therapist.

The therapist in a community center might work in a day-care program for the elderly or in a program for mentally disabled adults operated by a county recreation department. No matter what the disability, recreational therapists in community settings face the added logistical challenge of arranging transportation and escort services, if necessary, for prospective participants. Coordinating transportation is less of a problem in hospitals and nursing homes, where the patients all live under one roof. Developing therapeutic recreation programs in community settings requires a large measure of organizational ability, flexibility, and ingenuity.

REQUIREMENTS
High School
You can prepare for a career as a recreational therapist by taking your high school's college preparatory program. Naturally, this should include science classes, such as biology and chemistry, as well as mathematics and history classes. You can begin to gain an understanding of human behavior by taking psychology and sociology classes. For exposure to a variety of recreation specialties, take physical education, art, music, and drama classes. Verbal and written communication skills are essential for this work, so take English and speech classes. This job will require you to write reports, so computer science skills are also essential.

Postsecondary Training
Approximately 150 recreational therapy programs, which offer degrees ranging from the associate to the doctoral level, are currently available in the United States. While associate degrees in recreational therapy exist, such a degree will allow you only to work at the paraprofessional level. To be eligible for an entry-level professional position as a recreational therapist, you will need a bachelor's degree. Acceptable majors are recreational therapy, therapeutic recreation, and recreation with a concentration in therapeutic recreation. A typical four-year bachelor's degree program includes courses in both natural science (such as biology, behavioral science, and human anatomy) and social science (such as psychology and sociology). Courses more specific to the profession include programming for special populations; rehabilitative techniques including self-help skills, mobility, signing for the deaf, and

orientation for the blind; medical equipment; current treatment approaches; legal issues; and professional ethics. In addition, you will need to complete a supervised internship or field placement lasting a minimum of 480 hours.

Continuing education is increasingly becoming a requirement for professionals in this field. Many therapists attend conferences and seminars and take additional university courses. A number of professional organizations (for example, the National Therapeutic Recreation Society, the American Therapeutic Recreation Association, and the American Alliance for Health, Physical Education, Recreation and Dance) offer continuing education opportunities. Those with degrees in related fields can enter the profession by earning master's degrees in therapeutic recreation. Advanced degrees are recommended for those seeking advancement to supervisory, administrative, and teaching positions. These requirements will become more strict as more professionals enter the field.

Certification or Licensing
A number of states regulate the profession of therapeutic recreation. Licensing is required in some states; professional certification (or eligibility for certification) is required in others; titling is regulated in some states and at some facilities. In other states, many hospitals and other employers require recreational therapists to be certified. Certification is recommended for recreational therapists as a way to show professional accomplishment. It is available through the National Council for Therapeutic Recreation Certification. To receive certification you must meet eligibility requirements, including education and experience, as well as pass an exam. You are then given the title of certified therapeutic recreation specialist. Because of the variety of certification and licensing requirements, you must check with both your state and your employer for specific information on your situation.

Other Requirements
To be a successful recreational therapist, you must enjoy and be enthusiastic about the activities in which you involve your clients. You will also need patience and a positive attitude. Since this is people-oriented work, therapists must be able to relate to many different people in a variety of settings. They must be able to deal assertively and politely with other health care workers, such as doctors and nurses, as well as with the clients themselves and their families. In addition, successful therapists must be creative and have strong communication skills in order to develop and explain activities to patients.

Books to Read

Austin, David R. *Therapeutic Recreation: Processes and Techniques.* 5th ed. Champaign, Ill.: Sagamore Publishing, 2003.

Carter, Marcia Jean, Gary M. Robb, and Glen E. Van Andel. *Therapeutic Recreation: A Practical Approach.* 3d ed. Long Grove, Ill.: Waveland Press, 2003.

Dattilo, John. *Facilitation Techniques in Therapeutic Recreation.* State College, Pa.: Venture Publishing, 2000.

Heitzmann, Ray. *Careers for Sports Nuts & Other Athletic Types.* 3d ed. New York: McGraw-Hill, 2004.

Jensen, Clayne R., and Jay H. Naylor. *Opportunities in Recreation & Leisure Careers.* Rev. ed. New York: McGraw-Hill, 2005.

Stumbo, Norma, and Carol Ann Peterson. *Therapeutic Recreation Program Design: Principles and Procedures.* 4th ed. San Francisco: Benjamin Cummings, 2003.

Wilhite, Barbara, and Jean Keller. *Therapeutic Recreation: Cases and Exercises.* 2d ed. State College, Pa.: Venture Publishing, 2001.

EXPLORING

If you are interested in recreational therapy, you can find part-time or summer work as a sports coach or referee, park supervisor, or camp counselor. Volunteer work in a nursing home, hospital, or care facility for disabled adults is also a good way to learn about the daily realities of institutional living. These types of facilities are always looking for volunteers to work with and visit patients. Working with people with physical, mental, or emotional disabilities can be stressful, and volunteer work is a good way for you to test whether you can handle this kind of stress.

EMPLOYERS

Recreational therapists hold approximately 24,000 jobs, according to the U.S. Department of Labor. About 60 percent of these jobs are in nursing care facilities and hospitals. Other employers include residential facilities, adult day care centers, and substance abuse centers, and some therapists are self-employed. Employment opportunities also exist in long-term rehabilitation, home health care, correctional facilities, psychiatric facilities, and transitional programs.

STARTING OUT

There are many methods for finding out about available jobs in recreational therapy. A good place to start is the job notices and want ads printed in the local newspapers, bulletins from state park and recreation societies, and publications of the professional associations previously mentioned. State employment agencies and human service departments will know of job openings in state hospitals. College career services offices might also be able to put new recreational therapy graduates in touch with prospective employers. Internship programs are sometimes available, offering good opportunities to find potential full-time jobs.

Recent graduates should also make appointments to meet potential employers personally. Most colleges and universities offer career counseling services. Most employers will make themselves available to discuss their programs and the possibility of hiring extra staff. They may also guide new graduates to other institutions currently hiring therapists. Joining professional associations, both state and national, and attending conferences are good ways to meet potential employers and colleagues.

ADVANCEMENT

Newly graduated recreational therapists generally begin as *staff therapists*. Advancement is chiefly to supervisory or administrative positions, usually after some years of experience and continuing education. Some therapists teach, conduct research, or do consulting work on a contract basis; a graduate degree is essential for moving into these areas.

Many therapists continue their education but prefer to continue working with patients. For variety, they may choose to work with new groups of people or get a job in a new setting, such as moving from a retirement home to a facility for the disabled. Some may also move to a related field, such as special education, or sales positions involving products and services related to recreational therapy.

EARNINGS

Salaries of recreational therapists vary according to educational background, experience, certification, and region of the country. Recreational therapists had median earnings of $34,990 in 2006, according to the U.S. Department of Labor. The lowest paid 10 percent earned less than $20,880 a year, while the highest paid 10 percent earned more than $55,530 annually. Employment setting is also an important factor in determining salary. Recreational therapists employed by nursing care facilities earned mean incomes of $32,010, while those employed by general medical and surgical hospitals earned $40,030. Those in management positions command higher salaries. Supervisors report top salaries of $50,000 per year; administrators reported maximum earnings of $65,000 annually; and some consultants and educators reported even higher earnings.

Therapists employed at hospitals, clinics, and other facilities generally enjoy a full benefits package, including health insurance and vacation, holiday, and sick pay. Consultants and self-employed therapists must provide their own benefits.

WORK ENVIRONMENT

Working conditions vary, but recreational therapists generally work in a ward, a specially equipped activity room, or at a nursing home. In a community setting, recreational therapists may interview subjects and plan activities in an office, but they might work in a gymnasium, swimming pool, playground, or outdoors on a nature walk when leading activities. Therapists may also work on horse ranches, farms, and other outdoor facilities catering to people with disabilities.

The job may be physically tiring because therapists are often on their feet all day and may have to lift and carry equipment. Recreational therapists generally work a standard 40-hour week, although weekend and evening hours may be required. Supervisors may have to work overtime, depending on their workload.

OUTLOOK

The U.S. Department of Labor predicts that employment for recreational therapists will grow more slowly than the average for all occupations through 2014. Employment in nursing homes will grow slightly faster than in other areas. Fast employment growth is expected in assisted living, outpatient physical and psychiatric rehabilitation, and services for people with disabilities. Increased life expectancies for the elderly and for people with developmental disabilities such as Down's Syndrome will create opportunities for recreational therapists. The incidence of alcohol and drug dependency problems is also growing, creating a demand for qualified therapists to work in short-term alcohol and drug abuse clinics.

Most openings for recreational therapists will be in health care and assisted living facilities because of the increasing numbers and greater longevity of the elderly. There is also greater public pressure to regulate and improve the quality of life in retirement centers, which may mean more jobs and increased scrutiny of recreational therapists.

Growth in hospital jobs is not expected to be great. Many of the new jobs created will be in hospital-based adult day care programs or in units offering short-term mental health services. Because of economic and social factors, no growth is expected in public mental hospitals. Many of the programs and services formerly offered there are being shifted to community residential facilities for the disabled. Community programs for special populations are expected to expand significantly.

FOR MORE INFORMATION

For career information and resources, contact
American Association for Physical Activity and Recreation
1900 Association Drive
Reston, VA 20191-1598
Tel: 800-213-7193
Email: aapar@aahperd.org
http://www.aahperd.org/aapar

For career information, a list of colleges and universities that offer training, and job listings, contact
American Therapeutic Recreation Association
1414 Prince Street, Suite 204
Alexandria, VA 22314-2896
Tel: 703-683-9420
Email: atra@atra-tr.org
http://www.atra-tr.org

For information on certification, contact
National Council for Therapeutic Recreation Certification
7 Elmwood Drive
New City, NY 10956-5136
Tel: 845-639-1439
Email: nctrc@nctrc.org
http://www.nctrc.org

For career information, visit the NTRS under "Branches and Sections" on the Web site of the National Recreation and Park Association.

National Therapeutic Recreation Society (NTRS)
22377 Belmont Ridge Road
Ashburn, VA 20148-4501
Tel: 703-858-0784
Email: ntrsnrpa@nrpa.org
http://www.nrpa.org

Visit this Web site to find out about jobs, activities, schools, and other information related to the field.

Therapeutic Recreation Directory
http://www.recreationtherapy.com

Sport Psychologists

QUICK FACTS

School Subjects
Biology
Health
Psychology

Personal Skills
Communication/ideas
Helping/teaching

Work Environment
Primarily indoors
Primarily one location

Minimum Education Level
Master's degree

Salary Range
$35,280 to $59,440 to
$102,730+

Certification or Licensing
Required by all states

Outlook
Little or no change

DOT
045

GOE
12.02.02

NOC
4151

O*NET-SOC
19-3031.00, 19-3031.01,
19-3031.02

OVERVIEW

In general, *sport psychologists* work with amateur and professional athletes to improve their mental and physical health, as well as athletic performances, by using goal setting, imagery, focus strategies, and relaxation techniques, among others. Sport psychologists also strive to help athletes to mentally prepare for competition. There are approximately 179,000 psychologists employed in the United States, although sport psychologists comprise only a small segment of this number.

HISTORY

In the 17th century, French philosopher René Descartes described his belief that human behaviors could be classified in two ways—voluntary and involuntary. Behaviors completely mechanical, instinctual, and similar to those of animals, he characterized as involuntary; behaviors required or submitted to reason were characterized as voluntary. Based on this early model, and the subsequent work of others, including John Locke, James Mill, and John Stuart Mill, later philosophers and scientists experimented with sensation and perception, culminating with an introspective analysis of the many elements of an individual's experience.

William James advanced modern psychology by asserting the theory of a stream of thought; G. Stanley Hall, a contemporary of James, established the first true laboratory of psychology at Clark University in 1883. Sigmund Freud introduced the medical tradition to clinical psychology. A physician and neurologist, Freud's

126

methods of psychoanalysis included word association techniques and later, inkblot techniques as developed by Hermann Rorschach.

After World War II, psychology became formally recognized as a profession. The American Psychological Association has developed standards of training for psychologists, and certification and licensing laws have been passed to regulate the practice of professional psychology.

Since psychology deals with human behavior, psychologists apply their knowledge and techniques to a wide range of endeavors including human services, management, law, and sports.

THE JOB

Sport and exercise psychology is the scientific study of the psychological factors that are associated with participation and performance in sport, exercise, and other types of physical activity. In general, sport psychologists work with amateur and professional athletes to improve their mental and physical health, as well as athletic performances, by using goal setting, imagery, focus strategies, and relaxation techniques, among others. Sport psychologists also strive to help athletes to mentally prepare for competition.

Sport psychologists are divided into three categories: clinical, educational, and research. *Clinical sport psychologists* work mainly with individuals who are experiencing emotional problems that are usually, but not always, somehow connected to their sport. *Educational sport psychologists* have two roles, one as a classroom instructor and the other as a consultant. In the classroom, they teach students methods and techniques related to sport psychology. On the field, they usually function as members of the coaching staff. Just as the coach teaches physical skills, the sport psychologist teaches mental skills. *Research sport psychologists* conduct studies that provide the clinical and educational sport psychologists with scientific facts and statistics.

All sport psychology professionals are interested in two main objectives: helping athletes use psychological principles to improve performance (performance enhancement) and understanding how participation in sport, exercise, and physical activity affects an individual's psychological development, health, and well-being throughout the life span.

Sport psychologists work with individual athletes and entire teams. They may concentrate on the problems the athlete is having with the sport, from a bad slump to the feelings of low self-esteem that come when the crowd jeers the athlete's performance. Sport psychologists also work to help the individual athlete to overcome feelings of depression, drug or substance abuse, and violence.

They work with teams in many ways, the most notable of which is creating a feeling of cohesion among the many different personalities that constitute a team. Team members are also counseled when they are traded to another team or released.

Sport psychologists also work with individual athletes and team members on improving their level of performance, concentration, and mental attitude. The phrase "a winning attitude" derives its power from the fact that sport psychologists can help the athletes with whom they work to actually visualize a winning shot or a perfect golf swing and then execute that vision.

Sport psychologists don't work with only exceptional, elite athletes or teams; most sport psychologists, in fact, work with college athletes or amateur athletes, and many teach in academic settings or offer motivational lecture series. Some sport psychologists have their own columns in specialized sports magazines and others work in athletic training facilities, hired full time by the owners to work with the athletes who come there to train.

Sport psychology consultants provide many of the same services as sport psychologists but do not treat psychopathology (depression, eating disorders, drug addiction, etc.) since only licensed therapists and sport psychologists are qualified to do so. "A sport psychology consultant works on mental skills training with teams and individual athletes," says Carrie Cheadle, a sport psychology consultant in private practice in Northern California. "They help athletes work towards improving their physical performance by addressing the mental attributes necessary to be successful in sport. They address topics such as goal setting, relaxation, motivation, group dynamics, focus, etc. Many also address life skills (stress management, leadership, time management, etc.) as well." According to the Association for Applied Sport Psychology (AASP), sport psychology consultants typically work with a variety of individuals involved in sport and exercise, including athletes at all levels, athletes with disabilities, recreational athletes, injured athletes, exercise participants, group exercise leaders and personal trainers, health club instructors and administrators, coaches and administrators at all levels, and athletic trainers. Sport psychology consultants are also known as *mental skills coaches* and *performance enhancement consultants*.

REQUIREMENTS

The requirements for entering the field of sports medicine as a sport psychologist are somewhat tricky to understand, so it helps to understand the various paths available in psychology in general, as determined by the American Psychological Association. Students should expect to spend five to seven years in graduate work for a doctoral degree.

High School
High school students should take a college preparatory curriculum that concentrates on English, mathematics, and sciences. You should also take a foreign language, especially French and German, because reading comprehension of these languages is one of the usual requirements for obtaining a doctoral degree. Participation in sports will give you the background necessary to effectively understand the athletes you work with in your practice.

Postsecondary Training
A doctoral degree is generally required for employment as a psychologist, but there are two different degrees that psychologists can seek at the doctorate level. The first degree is called the Ph.D., and psychologists with this degree qualify for a wide range of teaching, research, clinical, and counseling positions in universities, elementary and secondary schools, and private industry. The second degree is called a Psy.D. (doctor of psychology); psychologists with this degree qualify mainly for clinical positions. The Ph.D. degree culminates in a dissertation based on original research, while the Psy.D. is usually based on practical work and examinations rather than a dissertation. In clinical or counseling psychology, the requirements for a doctoral degree usually include a year or more of internship or supervised experience.

Individuals who have only a master's degree in psychology are allowed to administer tests as psychological assistants and, if they are under the supervision of doctoral-level psychologists, they can conduct research in laboratories, conduct psychological evaluations, counsel patients, and perform administrative duties. They are also allowed to teach in high schools and two-year colleges and work as school psychologists or counselors.

Those individuals with only a bachelor's degree in psychology can assist psychologists and other professionals and work as research or administrative assistants, but without further academic training they cannot advance further in psychology.

Having said all of this, it will perhaps come as a shock that there are no sport psychology doctoral programs accredited by the American Psychological Association (APA). One of the controversies behind this is whether professionals working with athletes in applied areas of sport psychology should be required to have doctoral training in clinical or counseling psychology—training which would qualify them to provide psychological treatment to athletes as well. The solution reached by the APA, along with the Association for Applied Sport Psychology (AASP) and the North American Society for the Psychology of Sport and Physical Activity, is that any practitioners of sport psychology who do not also have doctoral-level clinical or counseling training should refer athletes who need treatment to licensed professionals. Sport psychologists who work with Olympic athletes are required to have doctoral-level degrees.

Those students who are interested in academic teaching and research in sport psychology can earn doctoral degrees in sport sciences and take additional courses in psychology or counseling. Over 50 schools in the United States offer this type of program, including the University of North Carolina–Greensboro (http://www.uncg.edu) and the University of Florida (http://www.ufl.edu). Typical subjects covered include sport psychology, performance enhancement, concentration skills, stress and attention management, and motivation.

Those students who want more emphasis on psychology in their training can pursue a psychology doctorate in areas such as group procedures, psychotherapy, learning, education, and human development or motivation, with a subspecialty in sport psychology. At most universities, students take courses like these in the sport sciences department, while at a few schools, such as the University of Washington (http://www.washington.edu) and the University of California–Los Angeles (http://www.ucla.edu), it is possible to take similar courses through the psychology department.

Students who wish to provide clinical services to athletes can pursue a doctoral degree in APA-accredited clinical or counseling psychology programs, with a concentration in sport psychology. This track offers students the widest range of job opportunities, from teaching and research in sports and psychology to counseling athletes as well as the general population. An institution where this mode of study is typical is the University of North Texas (http://www.unt.edu).

For those students who are interested primarily in educating people about the health benefits of exercise or in helping student athletes, a master's degree is an option. More than 100 sport sciences departments offer a master's degree in areas related to sport psychology.

For more detailed information on graduate programs in psychology and sport psychology, look for The Directory of Graduate Programs in Applied Sport Psychology, edited by Michael L. Sachs, Kevin L. Burke, and Diana C. Schrader (Morgantown, W. Va.: Fitness Information Technology, 2006).

Certification or Licensing

The AASP offers the certified consultant designation to members who meet educational requirements and accrue a specified number of hours of supervised experience in sport and exercise psychology.

Most states require that all practitioners of psychology meet licensing requirements if they are in independent practice or involved in offering patient care of any kind (including clinical and counseling). Once the educational requirements are fulfilled, a sport psychologist should contact the AASP for details about licensing requirements, as they usually vary from state to state.

Other Requirements

Because sport psychology is such a broad field, various personal attributes apply to different psychology positions. Clinical sport psychologists should be able to relate to others and have excellent listening skills. Educational sport psychologists should have strong communication skills in order to convey ideas and concepts to students and clients. Research sport psychologists should be analytical, detail oriented, and have strong writing and mathematics skills.

EXPLORING

You can gain experience in this field by volunteering to work for research programs at area universities or by working in the office of a psychologist. Another option is to learn more about sports by working as a gofer or intern with the sports medicine departments of college, university, or professional athletic teams. Even by participating in a sport in high school or college, you can gain valuable insight into the mental and emotional stresses and demands placed upon athletes.

In addition, students should begin their understanding of psychology by taking as many courses in the field as possible.

EMPLOYERS

Sport psychologists are employed by athletes at the amateur, college, or professional level and by owners of professional, college, and private organizations. They may also be employed at colleges and universities as teachers and researchers.

STARTING OUT

Along the road toward a Ph.D. or Psy.D., students of all levels can get involved in the research or educational aspects of psychology, either as a volunteer subject or a paid helper. These positions will gradually increase in responsibility and scope as the student progresses in his or her studies. Eventually, the student will be eligible for internships that will, in turn, provide him or her with valuable contacts in the field.

Graduates can explore job opportunities with a wide variety of employers, from the university research branch of psychology or sport sciences to the world of elite athletes. Finding work with the latter, however, can prove extremely difficult.

ADVANCEMENT

Sport psychologists advance in several ways, but primarily by increasing the scope and caliber of their reputations in the field. This is accomplished, of course, by consistently helping athletes to improve their athletic performance and to reduce the emotional and/or mental strain placed upon them. Advancement might come in the form of a new position (working for a professional team) or it might come in the form of a solid private practice.

Sport psychologists who make their living largely in the academic world do so by successfully publishing the results of studies, research, or theories in specialized medical journals.

EARNINGS

Specific salary figures for sport psychologists are not readily available. In general, psychologists' salaries depend on the area of their expertise, the location of their practice, and whether or not they practice alone or in a partnership. The U.S. Department of Labor reports that median annual earnings for all psychologists were $59,440 in 2006. The lowest paid 10 percent earned less than $35,280, and the highest paid 10 percent earned more than $102,730. Be forewarned, however, that with the higher salary comes long years of study in order to attain the educational background necessary to practice. In fact, in order to stay current with topics ranging from treatment to medication, psychologists must continue to learn and study their field for as long as they intend to practice.

WORK ENVIRONMENT

Sport psychologists spend most of their time working in office and hospital environments, but some of their time is spent in the same environments as the athletes they counsel. This may mean spending several hours on a golf course, on a ski slope, or in the gymnasium. Much depends on the type of psychologist. For example, the clinical psychologist would probably spend most of his or her time with athletes in the relative comfort of an office setting and the psychologist would meet with athletes during a regular nine-to-five day. Educational sport psychologists would be more likely to be in the gym or on the golf course, working side-by-side with the rest of the coaching staff. Depending on the nature of the study, a research sport psychologist might spend some time with athletes while they are practicing, but in general, he or she would spend most of the workday in an office or laboratory setting, reviewing or studying the data from his or her studies.

Sport psychologists need to stay up-to-date with developing theories and research. To accomplish this, they may have to spend additional time reading journals, books, and papers; conducting research in the library; or attending conferences on relevant issues. They may need to take additional course work to stay abreast of new theories and techniques, as well as to maintain current certification or licensing. Although sport psychologists spend a lot of time with the athletes they're helping, they also spend large amounts of time working alone.

OUTLOOK

While employment in the field of psychology in general is likely to grow faster than the average for all occupations through 2014, it is hard to say how this prognosis affects the subspecialty of sport psychology. Largely because so much time goes into the training, very few people leave the field entirely. Many stay in the general field of psychology and merely move around, switching specialties, but even this is rare.

While competition is incredibly tough for positions with elite athletes, most experts believe that other areas of sport psychology will continue to offer a substantial number of jobs to new graduates, especially in academe.

Sport psychology can lack the steady income of a private practice or academic teaching post because practitioners are frequently only on call, not steadily billing for their time. It can also be difficult to get work because while they might have a great, famous athlete for a client, chances are pretty good that the athlete doesn't want it known that he or she is getting counseling for a bad marriage, a slump, or a drug problem. This forces the sport psychologist to rely on referrals, which they may not receive all that often when athletes and their agents are trying to keep the athlete's therapy a secret.

FOR MORE INFORMATION

For information on career options in psychology, contact
American Psychological Association
Exercise and Sport Psychology Division
750 First Street, NE
Washington, DC 20002-4242
Tel: 800-374-2721
http://www.apa.org/divisions/div47

For certification info and an overview of the field, visit the About Applied Sport and Exercise Psychology section of the AASP Web site.
Association for Applied Sport Psychology (AASP)
2810 Crossroads Drive, Suite 3800
Madison, WI 53718-7942
Tel: 608-443-2475
http://www.aaasponline.org

For more information on sport psychology, contact
North American Society for the Psychology of Sport and Physical
    Activity
http://www.naspspa.org

═══════ INTERVIEW ═══════

Carrie Cheadle is a sport psychology consultant in private practice in Northern California. (Visit http://www.carriecheadle.com to learn more about her work.) Carrie discussed her career with the editors of Careers in Focus: Coaches and Fitness Professionals.

Q. What is the difference between a sport psychologist and a sport psychology consultant?

A. There are three types of sport psychology: clinical, educational, and research. My field falls under educational sport psychology. I have a bachelor of arts in psychology, a master of arts in sport psychology, and I am an Association for Applied Sport Psychology–certified consultant. I work with athletes to help them improve their physical sport performance through working on their mental skills and the psychological aspects of their performance. I don't treat psychopathology. A sport psychologist can also work with an athlete regarding issues of depression, general anxiety, eating disorders, drug addiction, etc.

Q. Please tell us about your business.

A. I have been consulting with athletes for six years. I have a private practice working with individual athletes both in person and via phone consulting. I also consult with teams, sport camps, and do workshops. I have worked with athletes in many different sports, but I specialize in working with cycling, triathlon, and endurance sports. I work with athletes of all ages and abilities, from recreational athletes to professional athletes competing at national and international levels. In addition to my private practice I also work for Stroke-Spine-Stride (http://www.diabetestrainingcamp.com), which is a fitness and training camp for people with diabetes, conducting the sport psychology component of the camp. I also teach undergraduate and graduate classes in sport psychology and supervise master's candidates.

Q. Why did you decide to become a sport psychology consultant?

A. After my undergraduate work in psychology, I was trying to figure out how to bridge my interest in psychology with helping people to perform to their potential, but I was having a hard time figuring out what that would be. I took some time off from school and moved to a mountain area to work in the ski industry and spent my spare time rock climbing and snowboarding. It was through my own sport experiences in those two sports, realizing what a huge impact my mind had on my performance, that I started to think about the psychology of performance. At that point, I didn't even know that sport psychology existed! It wasn't until my Mom told me about a graduate program in sport psychology that I realized it was something I could study and do as a profession.

Q. What is one thing that young people may not know about sport psychology?

A. The professional field of sport psychology has only been around for about 35 years; however, people have been researching the psychology of sport performance for over 100 years. The first research study was done in the late 1800s on cyclists. Now practitioners apply the principles of sport psychology and mental skills training with many different fields including dancers, musicians, theater arts, public speaking, police, armed forces, pilots, etc.

Q. What are the three most important professional qualities for sport psychology consultants?

A. There are *so many* important qualities that are essential to being an effective sport psychology consultant. I would say that the first quality is the ability to build rapport with your client. Whether you are working with one person or an entire team—you need to be able to build trust with your clients and create a relationship in order to effectively work together. The second quality is good communication skills. Effective communication means both speaking and listening. To be effective with speaking you need to be honest and know that the words you choose can impact your client. To be an effective listener you need to be completely absorbed in what your client is saying and not get distracted. You also need to be an active listener so your client can feel that they are being heard. The third quality is to have good assessment skills. You have to be able to assess your client's strengths and areas to improve before you can choose a plan of action.

Q. What do you like most and least about your job?

A. The thing that I like most and least about my job is the same thing! The professional field of sport psychology is a relatively new field, which means that at times it can be equally rewarding and challenging. The fact that the field is new means that it is a very exciting time to be a part of the progress and growth of the field. Sometimes I feel like I am a pioneer and helping pave the way for the future of sport psychology. However, because the field is new—part of my work is still dedicated to educating people on what exactly I do. Everyone knows what a firefighter is, what they do, and why their job is important. Right now, not everyone knows what a sport psychology consultant is, what they do, and why it's important.

Q. What is the future employment outlook in the field?

A. I think the future looks good. Professional organizations like the Association for Applied Sport Psychology (AASP) and The Exercise and Sport Psychology Division of the American Psychological Association (APA Division 47) are helping to develop the field and educate people on what defines an ethical and competent sport psychologist or sport psychology consultant. For any professional field to succeed, there need to be set standards of competence. The AASP has created a certification for consultants, setting a high standard of requirements in order to obtain certification. More and more athletes, coaches, and organizations are aware of sport psychology and how it can help enhance performance.

Sports Instructors and Coaches

OVERVIEW

Sports instructors demonstrate and explain the skills and rules of particular sports, like golf or tennis, to individuals or groups. They help beginners learn basic rules, stances, grips, movements, and techniques of a game. Sports instructors often help experienced athletes to sharpen their skills.

Coaches work with a single, organized team or individual, teaching the skills associated with that sport. A coach prepares her or his team for competition. During the competition, he or she continues to give instruction from a vantage point near the court or playing field.

HISTORY

Americans have more leisure time than ever and many have decided that they are going to put this time to good use by getting or staying in shape. This fitness boom, as well as a trend toward more sports competitions, has created employment opportunities for many sports-related occupations.

Health clubs, community centers, parks and recreational facilities, and private business now employ sports instructors who teach everything from tennis and golf to scuba diving.

As high school and college sports become even more organized, there continues to be a need for coaches qualified to teach the intricate skills associated with athletics today.

QUICK FACTS

School Subjects
English
Physical education

Personal Skills
Communication/ideas
Helping/teaching

Work Environment
Indoors and outdoors
Primarily multiple locations

Minimum Education Level
Some postsecondary training

Salary Range
$13,990 to $26,950 to
$5,000,000+

Certification or Licensing
Required in certain positions

Outlook
Faster than the average

DOT
153

GOE
01.10.01

NOC
5252

O*NET-SOC
27-2022.00

THE JOB

The specific job requirements of sports instructors and coaches varies according to the type of sport and athletes involved. For example, an instructor teaching advanced skiing at a resort in Utah will have different duties and responsibilities than an instructor teaching beginning swimming at a municipal pool. Nevertheless, all instructors and coaches are teachers. They must be very knowledgeable about rules and strategies for their respective sports. They must also have an effective teaching method that reinforces correct techniques and procedures so their students or players will be able to gain from that valuable knowledge. Also, instructors and coaches need to be aware of and open to new procedures and techniques. Many attend clinics or seminars to learn more about their sport or even how to teach more effectively. Many are also members of professional organizations that deal exclusively with their sport.

Safety is a primary concern for all coaches and instructors. Coaches and instructors make sure their students have the right equipment and know its correct use. A major component of safety is helping students feel comfortable and confident with their abilities. This entails teaching the proper stances, techniques, and movements of a game, instructing students on basic rules, and answering any questions.

A Little League coach teaches fielding techniques to his players. (*Jeff Greenberg, The Image Works*)

While instructors may tutor students individually or in small groups, a coach works with all the members of a team. Both use lectures and demonstrations to show students the proper skills, and both point out students' mistakes or deficiencies.

Motivation is another key element in sports instruction. Almost all sports require stamina, and most coaches will tell you that psychological preparation is every bit as important as physical training.

Coaches and instructors also have administrative responsibilities. College coaches actively recruit new players to join their team. Professional coaches attend team meetings with owners and general managers to determine which players they will draft the next season. Sports instructors at health and athletic clubs schedule classes, lessons, and contests.

REQUIREMENTS

Training and educational requirements vary, depending on the specific sport and the ability level of students being instructed. Most coaches who are associated with schools have bachelor's degrees. Many middle and high school coaches are also teachers within the school. Most instructors need to combine several years of successful experience in a particular sport with some educational background, preferably in teaching. A college degree is becoming more important as part of an instructor's background.

High School

To prepare for college courses, high school students should take courses that teach human physiology. Biology, health, and exercise classes would all be helpful. Courses in English and speech are also important to improve or develop communication skills.

There is no substitute for developing expertise in a sport. If you can play the sport well and effectively explain to other people how they might play, you will most likely be able to get a job as a sports instructor. The most significant source of training for this occupation is gained while on the job.

Postsecondary Training

Postsecondary training in this field varies greatly. College and professional coaches often attended college as athletes, while others attended college and received their degrees without playing a sport. If you are interested in becoming a high school coach, you will need a college degree because you will most likely be teaching as well as coaching. At the high school level, coaches spend their days teaching everything from physical education to English to mathematics, and so the college courses these coaches take vary greatly. Coaches of some youth league sports may not need a postsecondary degree, but they must have a solid understanding of their sport and of injury prevention.

Certification or Licensing

Many facilities require sports instructors to be certified. Information on certification is available from any organization that deals with the specific sport in which one might be interested.

Since most high school coaches also work as teachers, those interested in this job should plan to obtain teacher certification in their state.

Other Requirements

Coaches have to be experts in their sport. They must have complete knowledge of the rules and strategies of the game, so that they can creatively design effective plays and techniques for their athletes. But the requirements for this job do not end here. Good coaches are able to communicate their extensive knowledge to the athletes in a way that not only instructs the athletes but also inspires them to perform to their fullest potential. Therefore, coaches are also teachers.

"I think I'm good at my job because I love working with people and because I'm disciplined in everything I do," says Dawn Shannahan, former assistant girls' basketball and track coach at Leyden High School in Franklin Park, Illinois. Discipline is important for athletes, as they must practice plays and techniques over and over again. Coaches who cannot demonstrate and encourage this type of discipline will have difficulty helping their athletes improve. Shannahan adds, "I've seen coaches who are really knowledgeable about their sport but who aren't patient enough to allow for mistakes or for learning." Patience can make all the difference between an effective coach and one who is unsuccessful.

Similarly, Shannahan says, "A coach shouldn't be a pessimist. The team could be losing by a lot, but you have to stay optimistic and encourage the players." Coaches must be able to work under pressure, guiding teams through games and tournaments that carry great personal and possibly financial stakes for everyone involved.

EXPLORING

Try to gain as much experience as possible in all sports and a specific sport in particular. It is never too early to start. High school and college offer great opportunities to participate in sporting events as a player, manager, trainer, or in intramural leagues.

Most communities have sports programs such as Little League baseball or track and field meets sponsored by a recreation commission. Get involved by volunteering as a coach, umpire, or starter.

Talking with sports instructors already working in the field is also a good way to discover specific job information and find out about career opportunities.

EMPLOYERS

Besides working in high schools, coaches are hired by colleges and universities, professional sports teams, individual athletes such as tennis players, and by youth leagues, summer camps, and recreation centers.

STARTING OUT

People with expertise in a particular sport, who are interested in becoming an instructor, should apply directly to the appropriate facility. Sometimes a facility will provide training.

For those interested in coaching, many colleges offer positions to *graduate assistant coaches*. Graduate assistant coaches are recently graduated players who are interested in becoming coaches. They receive a stipend and gain valuable coaching experience.

ADVANCEMENT

Advancement opportunities for both instructors and coaches depend on the individual's skills, willingness to learn, and work ethic. A sports instructor's success can be measured by their students' caliber of play and the number of students they instruct. Successful instructors may become well known enough to open their own schools or camps, write books, or produce how-to videos.

Some would argue that a high percentage of wins is the only criteria for success for professional coaches. However, coaches in the scholastic ranks have other responsibilities and other factors that measure success; for example, high school and college coaches must make sure their players are getting good grades. All coaches must try to produce a team that competes in a sportsmanlike fashion regardless of whether they win or lose.

Successful coaches are often hired by larger schools. High school coaches may advance to become college coaches, and the most successful college coaches often are given the opportunity to coach professional teams. Former players sometimes land assistant or head coaching positions.

EARNINGS

Earnings for sports instructors and coaches vary considerably depending on the sport and the person or team being coached. The coach of a Wimbledon champion commands much more money per hour than the swimming instructor for the tadpole class at the municipal pool.

The U.S. Department of Labor reports that the median earnings for sports coaches and instructors were $26,950 in 2006. The lowest 10 percent earned less than $13,990, while the highest 10 percent earned more than $58,890. Sports instructors and coaches who worked at colleges and universities earned a mean annual salary of $44,200 in 2006, while those employed by elementary and secondary schools earned $27,550.

Much of the work is part time, and part-time employees generally do not receive paid vacations, sick days, or health insurance. Instructors who teach group classes for beginners through park districts or at city recreation centers can expect to earn around $6 per hour. An hour-long individual lesson through a golf course or tennis club averages $75. Many times, coaches for children's teams work as volunteers.

Many sports instructors work in camps teaching swimming, archery, sailing, and other activities. These instructors generally earn between $1,000 and $2,500, plus room and board, for a summer session.

Full-time fitness instructors at gyms or health clubs earned salaries that ranged from less than $14,880 to $56,750 or more per year in 2006, with a median salary of $25,910, according to the U.S. Department of Labor. Instructors with many years of experience and a college degree have the highest earning potential.

Most coaches who work at the high school level or below also teach within the school district. Besides their teaching salary and coaching fee—either a flat rate or a percentage of their annual salary—school coaches receive a benefits package that includes paid vacations and health insurance.

Head college football coaches at NCAA Division I schools earned an average of $950,000 a year in 2006, according to *USA Today*. A few top football coaches earn more than $2 million annually. Some top coaches in men's Division I basketball earn salaries of $1 million or more, according to *USA Today*. Women's basketball coaches at the college level typically earn lower salaries than their colleagues who coach men's sports—although top coaches earn salaries that are on par with coaches of men's basketball teams.

Coaches for professional teams often earn between $200,000 and $3 million. Some top coaches can earn more than $5 million annually. Many popular coaches augment their salaries with fees obtained from personal appearances and endorsements.

WORK ENVIRONMENT

An instructor or coach may work indoors, in a gym or health club, or outdoors, perhaps at a swimming pool. Much of the work is part time. Full-time sports instructors generally work between 35 and 40 hours per week. During the season when their teams compete, coaches can work 16 hours each day, five or six days each week.

It is not unusual for coaches or instructors to work evenings or weekends. Instructors work then because that is when their adult students are available for instruction. Coaches work nights and weekends because those are the times their teams compete.

One significant drawback to this job is the lack of job security. A club may hire a new instructor on very little notice, or may cancel a scheduled class for lack of interest. Athletic teams routinely fire coaches after losing seasons.

Sports instructors and coaches should enjoy working with a wide variety of people. They should be able to communicate clearly and possess good leadership skills to effectively teach complex skills. They can take pride in the knowledge that they have helped their students or their players reach new heights of achievement and training.

OUTLOOK

Americans' interest in health, physical fitness, and body image continues to send people to gyms and playing fields. This fitness boom has created strong employment opportunities for many people in sports-related occupations.

Health clubs, community centers, parks and recreational facilities, and private business now employ sports instructors who teach everything from tennis and golf to scuba diving.

According to the U.S. Department of Labor, these careers will grow faster than the average for all occupations through 2014. Job opportunities will be best in high schools and in amateur athletic leagues. Health clubs, adult education programs, and private industry will require competent, dedicated instructors. Those with the most training, education, and experience will have the best chance for employment.

The creation of new professional leagues, as well as the expansion of current leagues, will open some new employment opportunities for professional coaches, but competition for these jobs will be very intense. There will also be openings as other coaches retire, or are terminated. However, there is very little job security in coaching, unless a coach can consistently produce a winning team.

FOR MORE INFORMATION

For certification information, trade journals, job listings, and a list of graduate schools, visit the AAHPERD Web site.

American Alliance for Health, Physical Education, Recreation and Dance (AAHPERD)
1900 Association Drive
Reston, VA 20191-1598
Tel: 800-213-7193
http://www.aahperd.org

For information on membership and baseball coaching education, coaching Web links, and job listings, visit the ABCA Web site.

American Baseball Coaches Association (ABCA)
108 South University Avenue, Suite 3
Mount Pleasant, MI 48858-2327
Tel: 989-775-3300
Email: abca@abca.org
http://www.abca.org

For information on football coaching careers, contact

American Football Coaches Association
100 Legends Lane
Waco, TX 76706-1243
Tel: 254-754-9900
Email: info@afca.com
http://www.afca.com

For informational on hockey coaching, contact

American Hockey Coaches Association
7 Concord Street
Gloucester, MA 01930-2300
Tel: 781-245-4177
http://www.ahcahockey.com

For information on careers in sports and physical education, contact
National Association for Sport and Physical Education
1900 Association Drive
Reston, VA 20191-1598
Tel: 800-213-7193
Email: naspe@aahperd.org
http://www.aahperd.org/naspe

For information on basketball coaching, contact
National Association of Basketball Coaches
1111 Main Street, Suite 1000
Kansas City, MO 64105-2136
Tel: 816-878-6222
http://nabc.ocsn.com

For information on high school coaching opportunities, contact
National High School Athletic Coaches Association
PO Box 10065
Fargo, ND 58106-0065
Email: office@hscoaches.org
http://www.hscoaches.org

For information on the coaching of soccer, contact
National Soccer Coaches Association of America
6700 Squibb Road, Suite 215
Mission, KS 66202-3252
Tel: 800-458-0678
http://www.nscaa.com

Sports Physicians

OVERVIEW

Sports physicians, also known as *team physicians*, treat patients who have sustained injuries to their musculoskeletal systems during the play or practice of an individual or team sporting event. Sports physicians also do preparticipation tests and physical exams. Some sports physicians create educational programs to help athletes prevent injury. Sports physicians work for schools, universities, hospitals, and private offices; some also travel and treat members of professional sports teams.

HISTORY

The field of sports medicine, and nearly all the careers related to it, owes its foundation to experiments and studies conducted by Aristotle, Leonardo da Vinci, and Etienne Jules Marey. Aristotle's treatise on the gaits of humans and animals established the beginning of biomechanics. In one experiment, he used the sun as a transducer to illustrate how a person, when walking in a straight line, actually throws a shadow that produces not a correspondingly straight line, but a zigzag line. Leonardo da Vinci's forays into the range and type of human motion explored a number of questions, including grade locomotion, wind resistance on the body, the projection of the center of gravity onto a base of support, and stepping and standing studies.

However, it was Marey, a French physiologist, who created much more advanced devices to study human motion. In fact, sports medicine and modern cinematography both claim him as the father of their respective fields. Marey built the first force platform, a device

146

that was able to visualize the forces between the foot and the floor. Californian photographer Eadweard Muybridge's serial photographs of a horse in motion inspired Marey's invention of the chronophotograph. In contrast to Muybridge's consecutive frames, taken by several cameras, Marey's pictures with the chronophotograph superimposed the stages of action onto a single photograph; in essence, giving form to motion. By 1892, Marey had made primitive motion pictures, but his efforts were quickly eclipsed by those of film pioneers Louis and Auguste Lumiere.

Following both World Wars I and II, Marey's and other scientists' experiments with motion would combine with medicine's need to heal and/or completely replace the limbs of war veterans. To provide an amputee with a prosthetic device that would come as close as possible to replicating the movement and functional value of a real limb, scientists and doctors began to work together at understanding the range of motion peculiar to the human body.

Sports can be categorized according to the kinds of movements used. Each individual sport uses a unique combination of basic motions, including walking, running, jumping, kicking, and throwing. These basic motions have all been rigidly defined for scientific study so that injuries related to these motions can be better understood and treated. For example, sports that place heavy demands on one part of an athlete's body may overload that part and produce an injury, such as "tennis elbow" and "swimmer's shoulder." Baseball, on the other hand, is a throwing sport and certain injuries from overuse of the shoulder and elbow are expected. Athletes who play volleyball or golf also use some variation of the throwing motion and therefore sustain injuries to their shoulders and elbows.

Today, sports medicine concentrates on the treatment and prevention of injuries sustained while participating in sports. Sports medicine is not a single career but a group of careers that is concerned with the health of the athlete. For its specific purposes, the field of sports medicine defines *athlete* as both the amateur athlete who exercises for health and recreation, and the elite athlete who is involved in sports at the collegiate, Olympic, or professional level. Sports physicians treat people of all ages and abilities, including those with disabilities.

Among the professions in the field of sports medicine are the trainer, physical therapist, physiologist, biomechanical engineer, nutritionist, psychologist, and physician. In addition, the field of sports medicine also encompasses the work of those who conduct research to determine the causes of sports injuries. Discoveries made by researchers in sports medicine have spread from orthopedics to almost every branch of medicine.

Arthroscopic surgery falls into this category. It was developed by orthopedic surgeons to see and operate on skeletal joints without a large open incision. The arthroscope itself is a slender cylinder with a series of lenses that transmit the image from the joint to the eye. The lens system is surrounded by glass fibers designed to transfer light from an external source to the joint. Inserted into the joint through one small, dime- to quarter-sized incision, the arthroscope functions as the surgeon's "eyes" to allow pinpoint accuracy when operating. The surgical elements, themselves, are inserted through other small incisions nearby. In the 1970s only a few surgeons used the techniques of arthroscopy and did so as an exploratory measure to determine whether or not traditional surgery had a good chance of succeeding. Today, arthroscopy is the most commonly performed orthopedic surgery performed in the United States; instead of being an exploratory procedure, 80 percent of all arthroscopic surgeries are performed to repair tissue damage.

THE JOB

Sports physicians treat the injuries and illnesses of both the amateur and elite athlete. They are often referred to as team physicians. Depending upon the level of athlete they are treating, sports physicians are usually either practitioners in family practice as medical doctors (M.D.'s) or *orthopedic surgeons*. More often than not, the individual who works as the team physician for a professional sports team is too busy tending to the health needs of the team to have time for a private practice as well.

Brent Rich, M.D., team physician for Brigham Young University, agrees that there are some varieties of sports physicians: "Sports physicians come in two major varieties: primary care providers with training in nonsurgical sports medicine and orthopedic surgeons. The majority of sports physicians are in private practice. Each area has its rewards and downfalls. As a board-certified family physician, I deal with about 90 percent of what goes on in the sports medicine arena."

At the scholastic level, the team physician is usually the *school physician* and is appointed by the school board. Athletic programs at the collegiate level are usually capable of supporting a staff of one or more physicians who cater to the needs of the athletic teams. The size of the school and athletic program also determines the number of full-time physicians; for example, a state university basketball team might have one physician, even an orthopedic surgeon, dedicated wholly to that team's needs.

Professional teams, of course, have the necessary resources to employee both a full-time physician and an orthopedic surgeon. Generally, their presence is required at all practices and games. Often, professional teams have a sports medicine department to handle the various aspects of treatment, from training to nutrition to mental health. If they don't have their own department, they take advantage of the specialists at university hospitals and private care facilities in the area.

To fully understand the nature of a particular sports injury, sports physicians study the athlete as well as the sport. The musculoskeletal system is a complex organization of muscle segments, each related to the function of others through connecting bones and articulations. Pathological states of the musculoskeletal system are reflected in deficits (weaknesses in key muscle segments) that may actually be quite distant from the site of the injury or trauma. The risk factors for any given sport can be assessed by comparing the performance demands that regularly produce characteristic injuries with the risk factors that might predispose an athlete to injury.

Strength and flexibility, for example, are requirements for nearly every sport. Stronger muscles improve an athlete's performance, and deficits in strength can leave him or her prone to injury. Rehabilitation under the supervision of a sports physician focuses on rebuilding lost muscle strength. Likewise, an athlete who lacks flexibility may subject him or herself to strains or pulls on his or her muscles. For this athlete, rehabilitation would center on warming and stretching the isolated muscles, as well as muscle groups, to reduce or alleviate such muscle strains. In both cases, it is the responsibility of the sports physician to analyze the potential for injury and work with other sports health professionals to prevent it, as well as to treat the injury after it happens. The goal of every sports physician is to keep athletes performing to the best of their ability and to rehabilitate them safely and quickly after they are injured.

To prevent injuries, as well as treat them, sports physicians administer or supervise physical examinations of the athletes under their care to determine the fitness level of each athlete prior to that athlete actively pursuing the sport. During the exams, sports physicians note any physical traits, defects, previous injuries, or weaknesses. They also check the player's maturity, coordination, stamina, balance, strength, and emotional state. The physical examination accomplishes many different goals. To begin with, it quickly establishes the athlete's state of health and allows the sports physician to determine whether that athlete is physically capable of playing his or her sport. On the basis of the physical exam, the sports physician advises the coach on the fitness level of the athlete, which in turn determines a great deal about the athlete's position on the team. Furthermore, the exam alerts the sports physician to signs of injury, both old and new. Old or existing injuries can be noted and put under observation, and weaknesses can be detected early on so that coach and trainers can implement proper conditioning and training patterns.

Depending upon the results of their physical examinations, the sports physician may advise athletes to gain or lose weight, change their eating, drinking, and sleeping habits, or alter their training programs to include more strength or cardiovascular exercises. Routine physical checkups are also a common way of evaluating an athlete's performance level throughout a season, and many sports physicians will administer several exams to gauge the effect of their advice, as well as to ensure that the athlete is making the suggested changes in habits or training.

Preventing injuries is the sports physician's first goal and conditioning is probably the best way to accomplish that goal. Sports physicians are often responsible for developing and supervising the conditioning and training programs that other sports health professionals will implement. The sports physician may work with the coaching staff and athletic trainers to help athletes develop strength, cardiovascular fitness, and flexibility, or the sports physician may advise the coaching and training staff members of the overall safety of a practice program. For example, the sports physician may evaluate the drills and practice exercises that a football coach is using on a given day to make certain that the exercises won't exacerbate old injuries or cause new ones. Sports physicians may even be involved in the selection of protective gear and equipment. The degree of their involvement, again, depends on the size of the team and the nature of the physicians' skills or expertise, as well as on the number of other people on the staff. Large, professional teams tend to have equally large staffs on which one person alone is responsible for ordering and maintaining the protective gear.

Sports physicians are often in attendance at practices (or they are nearby, in case of an injury), but their presence at games is mandatory. If a player shows signs of undue fatigue, exhaustion, or injury, the sports physician needs to be there to remove the athlete from the competition. Dr. Rich says being at the games is one of the perks of his profession: "To see others accomplish what they desire gives me satisfaction. Another good part is covering sports events and feeling a part of the action on the sidelines, in the locker room, or in the heat of the battle."

After an athlete is injured, the sports physician must be capable of immediately administering first aid or other procedures. He or she first examines the athlete to determine the gravity and extent of the injury. If the damage is extreme enough (or cannot be determined from a manual and visual exam), the sports physician may send the athlete to the hospital for X rays or other diagnostic examinations. Later, the team physician may perform surgery or recommend that the athlete undergo treatment or surgery by a specialist. Some of the most common types of injuries are stress fractures, knee injuries, back injuries, shoulder injuries, and elbow injuries.

The sports physician oversees the athlete's recuperation and rehabilitation following an injury, including the nature and timing of physical therapy. The athlete's return to practice and competition is determined by the sports physician's analysis of the athlete's progress. Frequent physical examinations allow the physician to judge whether or not the athlete is fit enough to return to full activity. The decision to allow an athlete to compete again following an injury is a responsibility that sports physicians take seriously; whether the athlete is an amateur or an elite professional, the future health and well-being of the athlete is at stake and cannot be risked, even for an important championship game.

A developing area of the sports physician's responsibilities is the diagnosis and treatment of substance-abuse problems. Unfortunately, even as research on the field of sports medicine has produced new methods and medications that mask pain and decrease inflammation—which shortens recovery time and lengthens athletic careers—some also produce unnatural performance enhancement. Most notable of these are anabolic steroids—synthetic modifications of the male hormone, testosterone—which have become widely abused by athletes who use them to better their performances. When taken while on a high-protein diet and an intensive exercise regimen, these drugs can increase muscle bulk, which in turn can produce increased strength, speed, and stamina. The side effects of these drugs, however, include aggression, sterility, liver problems, premature closure of the growth plates of the long bones, and in women, male pattern baldness and facial hair. These side effects are usually irreversible and, as such, pose a significant health risk for young athletes.

Another method also banned from use in competition-level athletics is the withdrawal of an athlete's blood several weeks prior to competition. The blood is stored and then, just before the athlete competes, the blood is transfused back into his or her bloodstream. This process, blood doping, also has serious, even fatal, side effects, including heart failure and death.

Finally, professional athletes sometimes develop substance-abuse problems, such as alcohol or drug abuse. Sports physicians are responsible for detecting all of these problems and helping the athlete return to a healthy lifestyle, which may or may not include competing in their sport.

In addition to the responsibilities and duties outlined above, many sports physicians also perform clinical studies and work with researchers to determine ways of improving sports medicine practices. Often, the results of such studies and research are published in medical journals and popular magazines.

REQUIREMENTS

High School

During high school, take as many health and sports-related classes as possible. Biology, chemistry, health, computers, and English are important core courses. High grades in high school are important for anyone aspiring to join the medical profession, because competition for acceptance into medical programs at colleges and universities is always tough.

Postsecondary Training

Sports physicians have either an M.D. (medical doctor degree) or a D.O. (doctor of osteopathy degree). Each involves completing four years of college, followed by four years of medical school, study and internship at an accredited medical school, and up to six years of residency training in a medical specialty, such as surgery. Many physicians also complete a fellowship in sports medicine either during or after their residency.

During the first two years of medical school, medical students usually spend most of their time in classrooms learning anatomy, physiology, biology, and chemistry, among other subjects. In their last two years, they begin seeing patients in a clinic, observing and working with doctors to treat patients and developing their diagnostic skills. Some medical schools are beginning to alter this time-honored tradition by having medical students begin to work with patients much sooner than two years into their schooling, but this method of combining classroom and clinical experiences is not yet fully accepted or integrated into the curriculum.

After medical school, the new doctors spend a year in an internship program, followed by several years in a residency training program in their area of specialty. Most sports physicians complete this stage of their training by working in orthopedics or general practice.

The fellowship portion of a doctor's training is essential if he or she has chosen to specialize. For example, the doctor specializing in general surgery and interested in sports medicine would probably

seek an orthopedics fellowship providing further training in orthopedic surgery techniques.

Certification or Licensing

Sports physicians can become board certified in orthopaedic sports
medicine by the American Board of Orthopaedic Surgery. Contact
the board for more information on certification requirements.

To become licensed, doctors must have completed the above
training (detailed in Postsecondary Training) in accordance with
the guidelines and rules of their chosen area or specialty. Beyond
the formal requirements, this usually involves a qualifying written
exam, followed by in-depth oral examinations designed to test the
candidate's knowledge and expertise.

Other Requirements

To be a successful sports physician, you must be able to learn and
remember all the many parts of the human body and how they function together. Knowledge of different sports and their demands on
an athlete's body is also important. Like all medical doctors, you
need to be able to communicate clearly to your patients with compassion and understanding.

EXPLORING

High school students interested in becoming sports physicians should
look into the possibility of working with the physician, coach, or
athletic trainer for one of their school's teams. Firsthand experience
is the best way to gain fresh perspective into the role of the team
physician. Later on, when applying for other paid or volunteer positions, it will help to have already had sports-related experience. Dr.
Rich agrees, "Try to get experience with a physician who does what
you think you want to do. Spending time in their offices, in surgery,
or on the sidelines at high school games will give you exposure. As
you learn more, you can do more."

EMPLOYERS

Most sports physicians are in private practice, so they work for
themselves or with other medical doctors. Some sports physicians,
however, may work for sports clinics, rehabilitation centers, hospitals, and college/university teaching hospitals. Still other sports
physicians travel with professional baseball, basketball, football,
hockey, and soccer teams to attend to those specific athletes. Sports
physicians are employed all over the country.

STARTING OUT

You won't become the team physician for a National Basketball Association team fresh out of medical school. Many sports physicians begin by joining an existing practice and volunteering with a local sports organization. After several years they may apply to the school board for consideration as a team physician for their local school district. Later, they may apply for a position with a college team until they ultimately seek a position with a national or international professional athletics team or organization. This gradual climb occurs while the individual also pursues a successful private practice and builds a strong, solid reputation. Often, the sports physician's established reputation in an area of specialty draws the attention of coaches and management looking to hire a physician for their team. Others take a more aggressive and ambitious route and immediately begin applying for positions with various professional sports teams as an assistant team physician. As in any other field, contacts can prove to be extremely useful, as are previous experiences in the field. For example, a summer internship during high school or college with a professional hockey team might lead to a job possibility with that hockey team years later. Employment opportunities depend on the skill and ambitions of each job candidate.

ADVANCEMENT

Depending on the nature of an aspiring sports physician's affiliation with athletic organizations (part time or full time), advancement paths will vary. For most sports physicians, advancement will accompany the successful development of their private practices. For those few sports physicians employed full time by professional athletic organizations, advancement from assistant to team physician is usually accompanied by increased responsibilities and a corresponding increase in salary.

EARNINGS

The earnings of a sports physician vary depending upon his or her responsibilities and the size and nature of the team. The private sports physician of a professional individual athlete, such as a figure skater or long-distance runner, will most likely earn far less than the team physician for a professional football or basketball team, primarily because the earnings of the team are so much greater so the organization can afford to pay more for the physician's services. On the other hand, the team physician for the professional basketball team probably wouldn't have time for a private practice, although the sports physician for the figure skater or runner would, in all likelihood, also have a private practice or work for a sports health facility.

According to the U.S. Department of Labor, general practitioners and family practice physicians earned a mean income of approximately $149,850 in 2006. Ten percent of these physicians earned less than $69,990 annually in that same year, and some earned significantly more. This general figure does not include the fees and other income sports physicians receive from the various athletic organizations for whom they work. Again, these fees will vary according to the size of the team, the location, and the level of the athletic organization (high school, college, or professional, being the most common). The income generated from these fees is far less than what they earn in their private practices. On the other hand, those team physicians who are employed full time by a professional organization will likely make more than their nonprofessional sports counterparts, even as much as $1 million or more.

WORK ENVIRONMENT

Sports physicians must be ready for a variety of work conditions, from the sterile, well-lighted hospital operating room to the concrete bleachers at an outdoor municipal swimming pool. The work environment is as diverse as the sports in which athletes are involved. Although most of their day-to-day responsibilities will be carried out in clean, comfortable surroundings, on game day sports physicians are expected to be where the athletes are, and that might be a muddy field (football and soccer); a snow-covered forest (cross-country skiing); a hot, dusty track (track and field); or a steamy ring (boxing). Picture the playing field of any given sport and that is where you will find sports physicians. They are also expected to travel with the athletes whenever they go out of town. This means being away from their home and family, often for several days, depending on the nature, level, and location of the competition.

OUTLOOK

After years of watching athletes close down the bars after a game, coaches and management now realize the benefits of good health and nutrition. Within the world of professional sports, the word is out: Proper nutrition, conditioning, and training prevent injuries to athletes, and preventing injuries is the key when those athletes are making their owners revenues in the billions of dollars. A top sports physician, then, is a worthwhile investment for any professional team. Thus, the outlook for sports physicians remains strong.

Even outside the realm of professional sports, amateur athletes require the skills and expertise of talented sports physicians to handle the aches and pains that come from pulling muscles and overtaxing aging knees. Athletes of all ages and abilities take their competitions seriously, and are as prone to injury as any professional athlete, if not more, because amateur athletes in general spend less time conditioning their bodies.

FOR MORE INFORMATION

To obtain publications about sports medicine, contact
American College of Sports Medicine
PO Box 1440
Indianapolis, IN 46206-1440
Tel: 317-637-9200
http://www.acsm.org

To join a forum on various medical issues, visit the AMA Web site.
American Medical Association (AMA)
515 North State Street
Chicago, IL 60610-5453
Tel: 800-621-8335
http://www.ama-assn.org

For general information on sports medicine, contact
American Orthopaedic Society for Sports Medicine
6300 North River Road, Suite 500
Rosemont, IL 60018-4206
Tel: 847-292-4900
Email: aossm@aossm.org
http://www.sportsmed.org

For a list of accredited athletic training programs, job listings, and information on certification for athletic trainers, contact
National Athletic Trainers Association
2952 Stemmons Freeway
Dallas, TX 75247-6916
Tel: 214-637-6282
http://www.nata.org

Sports Trainers

OVERVIEW

Sports trainers, also referred to as *athletic trainers*, *certified sports medicine trainers*, and *certified sports medicine therapists*, help amateur and professional athletes prevent injuries, give first aid when an injury occurs during a practice or event, and manage the rehabilitation programs and routines of injured athletes.

Athletic trainers often consult with physicians during all stages of athletic training to ensure that athletes under their care are physically capable of participating in competition. In addition, they specialize in health care administration, education, and counseling. There are approximately 15,000 athletic trainers employed in the United States.

HISTORY

Aristotle, Leonardo da Vinci, and Etienne Jules Marey all conducted experiments and studies involving motion and the human body, but it was the 19th-century French physiologist Marey whose devices to study human motion really advanced the field of biomechanics and sports medicine. In fact, both modern cinematography and sports medicine claim him as the father of their respective fields. Marey's first contribution was the first force platform, a device that was able to visualize the forces between the foot and the floor. Marey's pictures with the chronophotograph superimposed the stages of action onto a single photograph; in essence, giving form to motion and allowing scientists to study it frame by frame, motion by motion. By 1892, Marey had even made primitive motion pictures, but his cinematic efforts were quickly eclipsed by those by Louis and Auguste Lumiere.

Following both World Wars I and II, Marey's and other scientists' experiments with motion would combine with the need to heal and/or completely replace the limbs of war veterans. In order to provide an amputee with a prosthetic device that would come as close as possible to replicating the movement and functional value of a real limb, scientists and doctors began to work together to understand the range of motion and interrelationships peculiar to each part of the human body.

Mechanically, sports can be categorized according to the kinds of movements used. Each individual sport utilizes a unique combination of basic motions, including walking, running, jumping, kicking, and throwing. These basic motions have all been rigidly defined for scientific study so that injuries related to these motions can be better understood and treated. For example, sports that place heavy demands on one part of an athlete's body may overload that part and produce an injury, such as tennis elbow and swimmer's shoulder. Baseball, on the other hand, is a throwing sport, and certain injuries from overuse of the shoulder and elbow are expected. Athletes who play volleyball or golf also use some variation of the throwing motion and therefore also sustain injuries to their shoulders and elbows.

Today, sports trainers are part of the team of sports medicine professionals that treat the injuries of both the amateur and elite athlete. Like sports physicians, certified sports trainers are responsible for preventing injuries as well as treating them, and they use their knowledge of the human body and its wide range of motions to discover new ways of reducing stress and damage from athletic activities. They work in high schools, secondary schools, colleges, and universities, and a smaller number work for professional teams. Many work in health clubs, sports medicine clinics, and other athletic health care settings. In 1990, the American Medical Association (AMA) recognized athletic training as an allied health profession.

THE JOB

Sports trainers help amateur and professional athletes prevent injuries through proper exercises and conditioning; provide immediate first-aid attention to injuries as they occur during a practice or event; and lead injured athletes safely through rehabilitation programs and routines. For the most part, sports trainers are not medical doctors and are not allowed to conduct certain procedures or provide advanced types of medical care, such as prescribing or administering drugs. Some trainers, however, are trained physicians. If an individual is also trained as an *osteopathic physician*, for example, he or she is licensed as a medical doctor and can conduct more advanced procedures and techniques, including diagnosis, surgery, and the prescription of drugs.

In order to prevent injuries, sports trainers organize team physicals, making certain that each player is examined and evaluated by a physician prior to that athlete's participation in the sport. Along with the team physician, they help to analyze each athlete's overall readiness to play, fitness level, and known or existing weaknesses or injuries. When necessary, they recommend stretching, conditioning, and strengthening exercises to aid the athlete in preventing or exacerbating an injury. This may involve developing specific routines for individual athletes. Finally, athletic trainers work with coaches, and sometimes team physicians, to choose protective athletic equipment. Before games and practice, they often inspect the playing field, surface, or area for any flagrant or subtle risks of injury to the athlete.

Prior to a practice or competition, the athletic trainer may help an athlete conduct special stretching exercises or, as a preventive measure, he or she might tape, wrap, bandage, or brace knees, ankles, or other joints, and areas of the athlete's body that might be at risk for injury. The trainer routinely treats cuts, scratches, and abrasions, among other minor injuries. He or she may tape, pad, or wrap injuries, and install face guards. When serious injuries do occur, whether in practice or during a competition, the athletic trainer's role is to provide prompt and accurate first-aid treatment to the athlete to ensure that athlete's full recovery. He or she is trained in emergency procedures and is prepared to provide emergency treatment for conditions such as shock, concussion, or bone fracture, stabilizing the athlete until they reach a hospital or trauma center. Often, the trainer will accompany the injured athlete to the hospital, making certain the team physician is still on hand to address the health concerns and needs of those athletes who are still competing.

Working in concert with the team physician and several other health professionals, athletic trainers often supervise the therapeutic rehabilitation of athletes under their care. They analyze the athlete's injury and create individualized therapy routines. Sometimes, the trainer may advise the athlete to wear a protective brace or guard to minimize damage while the athlete is recuperating from an injury. Athletic trainers in charge of every level of athlete should be licensed to perform specific medical functions and operate certain devices and equipment.

REQUIREMENTS

High School

If you have an interest in becoming a sports trainer, you've probably already become involved in the field during high school. Maybe you're not an athlete but you work as a trainer or manager for one of your school's teams. These are excellent ways to develop your interest in sports, learn about the skills that trainers must have, and develop the leadership abilities necessary for the job.

If you're interested in this field, you should pay special attention to physical education classes and to high school subjects such as health and anatomy and physiology. Students with an interest in becoming athletic trainers will want to become certified in CPR and first aid.

Postsecondary Training

Sports trainers usually earn a bachelor's degree from a college or university that òffers a program in athletic training that is accredited by the Commission on Accreditation of Athletic Training Education (http://caate.net). Many students go on to earn a master's degree in athletic training. More than 70 percent of certified athletic trainers have at least a master's degree, according to the National Athletic Trainers' Association (NATA). Students then intern with a certified athletic trainer. Another option is to earn a bachelor's degree or a master's degree in a related health field, such as osteopathy, and then intern with a certified athletic trainer. The number of hours you need to spend in both clinical study and in the internship phase will vary, depending on the program you select and the professional organization that you decide to join.

Most accredited programs in athletic training include course work in the prevention and evaluation of athletic injuries and illnesses, first aid and emergency care, therapeutic exercises, therapeutic modalities, administration of athletic training programs, human anatomy, human physiology, exercise physiology, kinesiology, nutrition, psychology, and personal and community health.

Certification or Licensing

As mentioned earlier, athletic trainers in charge of every level of athlete should be licensed to perform specific medical functions and operate certain devices and equipment. Different membership organizations and their respective certifying bodies have different eligibility requirements; it is up to you to decide which organization best characterizes your ultimate goal.

For example, NATA requires that each member have a bachelor's degree (in any field), be either a graduate of an accredited program in athletic training (with 800 clinical hours) or complete an internship (with 1,500 clinical hours), and pass a certification exam consisting of three sections—written, simulation, and oral practical.

Approximately 43 states require some form of certification, licensure, or registration for athletic trainers. For more information, check with your state's regulatory agency in the state in which you would like to practice for more information.

Other Requirements

Workers in this field need an understanding of human anatomy and physiology, both in terms of physical capabilities and injury treatment and prevention. You should not be squeamish when it comes to blood, broken bones, or other wounds. Athletes do get hurt, and a trainer who is unable to cope well with this aspect of sports may have a difficult time succeeding in the career. The ability and knowledge to handle medical emergencies is especially important for certified athletic trainers, whose work focuses on injury prevention and treatment.

EXPLORING

Most trainers, like other professionals who work with athletes, were first drawn to sports as participants. High school and college students can gain valuable experience by actively participating in a sport. Such experience lends a prospective trainer added insight into the injuries typical of a given sport, as well as the compassion and empathy necessary to comfort an injured athlete forced to sit out a game. Most teams need help with everything from equipment to statistics, so plenty of opportunities exist to explore a variety of sports-related positions. If you are certain about becoming an athletic trainer, you can often work with and learn beside a trainer or team physician. This type of experience will come in handy later, when you are looking for an internship or a job; successful candidates are usually those with the most experience and on-the-job training.

EMPLOYERS

Approximately 15,000 athletic trainers are employed in the United States. Trainers are employed by professional and amateur sports teams, private sports organizations, sports facilities, educational institutions, and by individual athletes. Other possible athletic-training employment opportunities can be found in corporate health programs, health clubs, clinical and industrial health care programs, and athletic training curriculum programs.

STARTING OUT

Athletic trainers, regardless of the professional organization they join, are usually required to complete a period of training with a certified athletic trainer or sports medicine therapist. These internships provide students with the foundation for future networking possibilities. Many students find full-time jobs with the teams, organizations, or school districts with which they interned. At the very least, these internships offer students the chance to make valuable contacts and gain valuable on-the-job experience.

Most accredited programs in athletic training also have job placement departments that host recruitment seminars with major organizations, provide career counseling services, and put students in contact with prospective employers.

Finally, one of the benefits to belonging to a professional organization is that these associations publish newsletters and maintain Web sites, both of which list job openings. Some organizations even offer job hotlines to their members. Through these media, as well as through meetings, seminars, and continuing education, students and trainers can make new contacts that will help them locate work and add to their base of knowledge. NATA, for example, boasts the most comprehensive job referral service in the United States for athletic trainers, listing job openings in all athletic training settings and locations.

ADVANCEMENT

Acquiring additional training and education is the most common way of advancing in the field of sports training. Those trainers who have spent years working in the field and who update their skills each year by taking continuing education courses, sometimes even returning to school for an advanced degree, will be among the first to receive promotions.

Management responsibilities are the other way in which athletic trainers can advance in their field. Large universities often employ several trainers to serve the many different teams, with one trainer acting as the head trainer, sometimes also called the director of sports medicine. This individual coordinates the daily activities and responsibilities of the other trainers and works closely with the coaches of the school's various teams to ensure that all the demands are being met. Most often, trainers advance by working for several years at one school and then move on to another school when an opening is announced that will mean greater responsibilities and benefits.

EARNINGS

Earnings vary depending on the level of athletics in which the trainer is involved, the trainer's education and credentials, and the number and type of his or her responsibilities. Those considering a career as an athletic trainer should keep all aspects of the job and salary in per-

Mean Annual Earnings by Specialty, 2006

Spectator sports	$46,350
Elementary and secondary schools	$45,230
Business, professional, labor, political, and similar organizations	$44,680
Colleges, universities, and professional schools	$41,340
General medical and surgical hospitals	$39,330
Offices of other health practitioners	$36,640

Source: U.S. Department of Labor

spective; the slight increase in salary of a trainer working for a college team might be offset by the higher stress levels and longer hours away from home. Trainers who work with professional athletes are away from home a great deal, including evenings, weekends, and holidays.

According to the National Association for Sport and Physical Education, salaries for athletic trainers in schools range from $25,000 to $35,000. With experience and a master's degree, college trainers can earn up to $45,000 to $60,000 per year. Athletic trainers who work for professional sports teams earn salaries ranging from $60,000 to $125,000.

The U.S. Department of Labor reports that athletic trainers earned median salaries of $36,560 in 2006. The highest 10 percent earned more than $57,580, while the lowest 10 percent earned less than $21,940.

WORK ENVIRONMENT

Athletes train year round and so do the sports trainers who supervise their conditioning and rehabilitation programs. Depending upon the level and size of an athletic program, trainers may work with athletes in one or more sports. Sports trainers who work in high schools often act as the trainer for several, or all, of the athletic teams. A lot also depends on the school's budgetary restrictions. Generally speaking, though, most schools have a separate trainer for men's and women's sports. Trainers in professional sports work only in one sport and for one team.

Most of the trainer's time is spent in the school's athletic facility, either in preparation for work or in conditioning or rehab sessions.

Athletic trainers are on a schedule similar to that of their athletes; they go to practices, schedule weight and rehab sessions, and attend games. They are expected to travel when and where the team travels.

OUTLOOK

The U.S. Department of Labor predicts that athletic trainers will experience much faster than average job growth throughout 2014. The increasing number of amateur and school sports teams accounts for some of this growth, as does the public's increasing interest in health and fitness. Competition for the more glamorous jobs is tough; positions with professional athletes and teams are extremely difficult to find and those working in them usually have years and years of experience. More opportunities exist for certified athletic trainers who work with high school athletes, especially if trainers have other skills that make them more employable. For example, the athletic trainer wishing to work with high school athletes who also can teach biology, math, physical education, or other school subjects most likely will find a position sooner than the candidate with only a background in athletic training. The reasoning is simple: with school budgets being cut back, those individuals who perform double-duty will be more attractive to school boards looking to cut costs.

Positions at the college and university level offer the athletic trainer greater stability, with little turnover. Competition for these spots is also tough, however, and many schools are now requiring candidates to have a master's degree in order to be considered.

FOR MORE INFORMATION

To obtain publications about sports medicine, contact
    American College of Sports Medicine
    PO Box 1440
    Indianapolis, IN 46206-1440
    Tel: 317-637-9200
    http://www.acsm.org

For information on certification, contact
    Board of Certification Inc.
    4223 South 143rd Circle
    Omaha, NE 68137-4505
    Tel: 877-262-3926
    Email: staff@nataboc.org
    http://www.bocatc.org

For a list of accredited athletic training programs, job listings, and information on certification, contact

National Athletic Trainers' Association
2952 Stemmons Freeway
Dallas, TX 75247-6916
Tel: 214-637-6282
Email: ebd@nata.org
http://www.nata.org

Strength and Conditioning Coaches

QUICK FACTS

School Subjects
Health
Physical education

Personal Skills
Communication/ideas
Helping/teaching

Work Environment
Indoors and outdoors
Primarily multiple locations

Minimum Education Level
Bachelor's degree

Salary Range
$13,990 to $44,200 to
$100,000+

Certification or Licensing
Recommended

Outlook
Faster than the average

DOT
153

GOE
01.10.01

NOC
5252

O*NET-SOC
27-2022.00

OVERVIEW

Strength and conditioning coaches help athletes attain optimum performance through strength training, exercise, and nutritional programs. They work with athletes at all levels, as well as members of the general public who wish to improve their strength, speed, agility, and endurance.

HISTORY

Strength and conditioning coaching evolved as a distinct career path in the 1970s when collegiate and professional sports programs began looking for ways to increase the performance and competitiveness of their athletes. Soon after, high schools, as well as individual athletes, also began seeking the services of strength and conditioning coaches to help improve athletic performance. Today, strength and conditioning coaches are key members of athletic programs.

The National Strength and Condition Association (NSCA) was formed in 1978 to represent the professional interests of strength and conditioning coaches at all levels. It has approximately 30,000 members.

The Collegiate Strength & Conditioning Coaches Association (CSCCa) was founded in 2000. While it primarily represents coaches at the collegiate level, it recently began offering membership to coaches of professional athletic teams.

THE JOB

It's no longer enough for an athlete to rely on natural athletic ability. Most athletes turn to strength and conditioning coaches to bring them to the top of their game. Such coaches are responsible for identifying an athlete's weaknesses, and creating a conditioning plan to improve strength, form, speed, agility, and endurance.

The conditioning plan will be determined based on the individual athlete, and the sport in question. For example, basketball players may require workouts for stronger leg muscles and core, while golfers may concentrate on more powerful arm and shoulder muscles. The first step is a thorough assessment of the athlete. Equipment such as treadmills, free weights, and weight machines may be used to gauge speed and strength. Oftentimes, the athlete is hooked up to an EKG machine in order to measure his or her heart rate during the workout. Other equipment and technology may also be used to assess the health and overall conditioning level of the athlete.

After the initial assessment, coaches design and implement a sport-specific program while addressing the goals of each athlete. The time of year, whether or not the sport is in season, may also play a part in designing the program. Conditioning sessions may be scheduled more frequently during the off-season when players do not have regular team practices and games. Coaches use their knowledge of anatomy, physiology, and kinesiology to suggest exercises to develop strong leg muscles, powerful arm muscles, a strong core, and cardiovascular endurance. These exercises may include free weights, stationary weight machines, and bands. Coaches supervise all sessions to ensure exercises are performed properly. This may prove demanding at times, especially if the coach is responsible for managing several athletes at one time. Coaches may prescribe plyometrics, or explosive movement exercises, to develop muscular power, which in turn improves an athlete's speed and agility. In addition to building muscle strength, coaches also make sure athletes are in top form in order to avoid injury. They may monitor an athlete's nutrition regimen, and suggest changes in diet or lifestyle.

A coach who oversees an entire strength and conditioning program is known as the *lead coach* or the *head strength and conditioning coach*. Depending on the size of the athletic program, they may supervise one or more assistant coaches to help with physical fitness and development. This is especially true if the strength and conditioning coaches are responsible for multiple sports disciplines. The lead coach is also responsible for managing the fitness facility, budgeting for new equipment, overseeing the maintenance and repair of existing equipment, and hiring assistants as needed. They also work closely with head coaches to ensure that specific strength and conditioning goals are met.

REQUIREMENTS

High School

To prepare for this career, take courses in human physiology, exercise science, biology, and health in high school. Additionally, courses in English and speech will also help you develop your communication skills.

Postsecondary Training

Strength and conditioning coaches have a variety of educational backgrounds. Most earn a bachelor's degree in physical education, kinesiology, exercise physiology, or a related area. The NSCA recognizes collegiate strength and conditioning or sport performance programs that have met educational guidelines established by the association. Visit http://nsca-lift.org/ERP to learn more. Some top employers may require strength and conditioning coaches to have a master's degree.

Certification or Licensing

The NSCA offers the certified strength and conditioning specialist designation to applicants who pass a rigorous examination. Contact the association for more information.

The CSCCa offers two levels of voluntary certification. Coaches who have a bachelor's degree, pass an examination, have certification in CPR, and satisfy other requirements are eligible for the strength and conditioning coach certified designation. Those who have worked as full-time, collegiate and/or professional strength and conditioning coaches for a minimum of 12 years, have earned the strength and conditioning coach certified designation, and satisfy other requirements may receive the master strength and conditioning coach designation.

Some employers may require that strength and conditioning coaches be certified in CPR.

Other Requirements

Coaches must be experts regarding weight training, conditioning, nutrition, and exercise. They must also be strong communicators in order to effectively educate athletes regarding the benefits of weight training and conditioning, as well as communicate with other coaching professionals regarding the performance and conditioning of athletes. Coaches must be willing to work long hours when their teams compete, and be willing to learn about new strength and conditioning techniques throughout their careers.

EXPLORING

You can learn more about strength and conditioning coaching by visiting the Web sites of college and professional sports teams. The CSCCa offers a list of college strength and conditioning programs at its Web site, http://nsca-lift.org/CSCW/default.asp. You can also read industry publications such as *Strength and Conditioning Journal* and the *Journal of Strength and Conditioning Research;* both journals are published by the NSCA. Talk to your physical education teacher and sports coaches about strength and conditioning training, and ask them to arrange an information interview with a professional in the field. Volunteer to work as a coach for one or more of your high school sports teams.

EMPLOYERS

The majority of employment opportunities exist at the professional or collegiate levels. All professional and collegiate teams, from baseball to soccer to football, have strength and conditioning coaches on staff. Employers at this level expect candidates to have a master's degree in a health science, as well as work experience. Those holding a bachelor's degree and having little work experience may still find employment, but only at an assistant's level.

Coaches working with high school teams may be required to hold an education degree as some schools require their coaching staff to teach classes as well as condition athletes.

A growing number of employment opportunities can be found with private clients. Many intramural teams encourage their players to attend camps to work on speed, agility, and overall fitness. Such companies offer private sessions and group camps to help athletes from many different sport backgrounds improve their overall sports performance. They tailor their programs to meet the specific demands of each sport. Their clientele includes adults as well as children as young as 11 years old.

STARTING OUT

Participating in an internship program while in college is an excellent way to make contacts and land your first job in the field. Internships may be arranged by your college or offered by professional associations. The NSCA and the CSCCa both offer internship programs to student members. Additionally, both the NSCA and the CSCCa offer job listings at their Web sites (see For More Information).

Did You Know?

- Strength training can help people increase their cardiovascular health by maintaining or increasing lean body mass and producing slight decreases in the relative percentage of body fat. It also increases bone mineral density and may delay or prevent osteoporosis.
- Strength training may reduce depression and anxiety and encourage overall psychological well-being.
- The number of adults who strength trained two or more times a week increased from 17.7 percent in 1998 to 19.6 percent in 2004. While this is an improvement, it still falls short of the 30 percent objective for 2010 established by the President's Council on Physical Fitness and Sports and the Centers for Disease Control and Prevention.

Sources: Centers for Disease Control and Prevention, National Strength and Conditioning Association

ADVANCEMENT

Advancement for strength and conditioning coaches depends on the individual's position, skills, and work ethic. Success for coaches can also be quantified by the success of the individuals they coach (for example, a basketball player who is able to double his or her playing time and scoring because he or she is in better condition), the number of athletes they coach (advancing to coach college athletes in multiple sports), or the type of employer (moving from the collegiate level to employment as a coach for a Major League Baseball team). Some coaches may advance by becoming well known enough to write books or produce how-to videos. Others may become college professors.

EARNINGS

Earnings for strength and conditioning coaches vary considerably depending on the sport and the person or team being coached. The U.S. Department of Labor reports that the median earnings for all sports coaches and instructors were $26,950 in 2006. The lowest 10 percent earned less than $13,990, while the highest 10 percent earned more than $58,890. Sports instructors and coaches who worked at colleges and universities earned a mean annual salary of $44,200 in 2006, while those employed by elementary and secondary schools earned $27,550. Strength and conditioning coaches who are employed by colleges and universities might earn salaries that range from $35,000 to $70,000 annually, while coaches at the professional level can earn more than $100,000 a year.

WORK ENVIRONMENT

Strength and conditioning coaches may work indoors, in a gym or health club, or outdoors, perhaps at a swimming pool. Coaches for collegiate and professional sports teams may work 50 to 60 hours a week (including evenings), six to seven days a week when athletes are in competition.

OUTLOOK

According to the U.S. Department of Labor, employment for all coaches is expected to grow faster than the average for all occupations through 2014. Strength and conditioning coaches will be increasingly relied on to provide athletes with the extra edge during competition. Despite this prediction, there will be strong competition for positions—especially at the collegiate and professional levels. Strength and conditioning coaches who are certified and who have considerable experience will have the best chances for employment.

FOR MORE INFORMATION

For information on internships, job opportunities, and certification, contact
Collegiate Strength & Conditioning Coaches Association
PO Box 7100
University Station
Provo, UT 84602-7100
Tel: 801-375-9400
http://www.cscca.org

For information on strength and conditioning in the sport of football, contact
Football Strength and Conditioning Coaches Society
42 Green Hill Drive
Covington, LA 70448
Tel: 985-893-1855
http://www.prostrengthcoach.com

For information on careers in sports and physical education, contact
National Association for Sport and Physical Education
1900 Association Drive
Reston, VA 20191-1598
Tel: 800-213-7193
Email: naspe@aahperd.org
http://www.aahperd.org/naspe

For information on certification, scholarships, and the field, contact
National Strength and Conditioning Association
1885 Bob Johnson Drive
Colorado Springs, CO 80906-4000
Tel: 800-815-6826
http://www.nsca@nsca-lift.org

Yoga and Pilates Instructors

OVERVIEW

Yoga and pilates instructors lead specialized exercise, stretching, and meditation classes for people of all ages. They demonstrate techniques in front of the class and then watch members perform the movements, making suggestions and form adjustments as needed. Classes range from introductory to intermediate to advanced, and they may be aimed at specific groups, such as children or the elderly. *Yoga instructors* lead their class through a series of asanas, or poses, aimed at building strength, flexibility, and balance. *Pilates instructors* teach a series of movements that are more fluid than the poses used in yoga. Pilates also builds strength and flexibility but focuses on training the individual's core, or center.

HISTORY

Yoga and pilates have existed in other cultures for many years, but they have become more popular in the United States only in the last few decades.

Yoga, which literally means to yoke together, is an ancient practice. According to the American Yoga Association, early stone carvings and illustrations dating back 5,000 years reveal depictions of people in yoga positions. Contrary to popular belief, yoga is not rooted in Hinduism. In fact, Hinduism was established much later, and early Hindu leaders adopted and promoted certain yoga beliefs and practices for their followers.

One of the earliest known yoga teachers and promoters was a man named Patanjali, who wrote about his yoga practice in a work called *Yoga Sutras*. His writings covered the basic philosophy and techniques that later became hatha yoga. Within hatha are many styles, such as Iyengar, Ashtanga, Integral, Kripalu, and Jiva Mukti. Ashtanga yoga, one of the most popular branches, incorporates eight elements: restraint, observance, breathing exercises, physical exercises, preparation for meditation, concentration, meditation, and self-realization. Most modern yoga instructors focus on just a few of these elements, leading classes through physical poses, breathing techniques, and preparation for meditation.

Pilates (pronounced puh-lot-eez) was developed by Joseph Pilates in the early 1900s. A German living in England during the start of World War I, Pilates was forced into a camp with other foreign nationals. During this time, Pilates encouraged his fellow cellmates to keep moving, even those who were bedridden. According to Katherine Robertson, author of *Pilates...the Intelligent, Elegant, Workout*, Joseph Pilates developed exercise equipment specifically for the injured, converting hospital beds to "bednasiums," which encouraged health and healing through resistance exercise.

This early rehabilitation work led to the machinery behind pilates exercise. In addition to floor work, Joseph Pilates also incorporated complex equipment consisting of belts, loops, chains, and springs designed to strengthen and lengthen the core muscles of the body.

Today, pilates is still practiced in its original form, with both mat work and equipment, though many instructors, because of the cost of equipment, offer classes consisting of just floor exercises.

THE JOB

Yoga and pilates instructors teach alternatives to the more traditional exercises of aerobics, weight training, or interval training classes. With yoga, the instructors' methods vary greatly based on the type of yoga they teach. Some instructors begin class seated or even lying down, encouraging class members to relax their muscles and focus on their breathing. After a few minutes of breathing exercises, the instructor leads the class into the various asanas, or yoga poses. These poses have Sanskrit names, though the instructor may use the English terminology for the benefit of the class, instructing students to get into the downward dog position or child's pose. Again, depending on the yoga method, poses may be fluid, with quicker movement from position to position, or instructors may tell class members to hold poses for as long as three or four minutes, encouraging strength and control.

A pilates instructor works with a client. *(Rick Gomez, Corbis)*

Most yoga classes are done barefoot on the floor, using a thin, rubber mat to keep class members from slipping while in poses. Other equipment, such as foam blocks, ropes, or cloth straps, may also be used in the poses, usually to help with form or assist in the tougher positions.

During the class, yoga instructors verbally describe and demonstrate moves in front of the class. They also walk around and survey the movements of class members, making slight adjustments to members' form to prevent injury, encourage good practice, and improve their skills.

Pilates is similar to yoga in that class participants are led through different motions. However, unlike yoga poses that are often held for minutes at a time, pilates encompasses more fluid movement of the arms and legs using what is called core strength. This strength comes from the body's torso, from the top of the rib cage to the lower abdomen.

The job of a pilates instructor is similar to that of a yoga teacher. Pilates teachers also demonstrate and describe motions and check class members' form and technique. Some classes include equipment such as an apparatus called The Reformer, which is a horizontal framework of straps and springs that is used for more than 100 exercises. Class members can tone, build, lengthen, and strengthen muscles by adjusting the equipment's springs to create different levels of resistance.

Both yoga and pilates instructors have to prepare for their classes ahead of time to choose the exercises and equipment to be used or whether to focus on one method or area of the body. Good instructors are available after class for questions and advice. Instructors should also be open to class suggestions and comments to make the class the best it can be.

REQUIREMENTS

High School

You will need at least a high school diploma to work as a yoga or pilates instructor. In high school, take anatomy, biology, psychology, and physical education. In addition, get involved in weight lifting, dance, sports, and other activities that will help you to stay fit and learn more about exercise.

Postsecondary Training

Although a college degree isn't always necessary to work in the fitness field, you will be more attractive to employers if your qualifications contain a balance of ability and education. Useful college courses include anatomy, physiology, psychology, kinesiology, biomechanics, chemistry, physics, first aid and safety, health, and nutrition.

Certification or Licensing

Most qualified yoga and Pilates instructors become certified through a professional association, such as the Yoga Alliance or The Pilates Center. For example, The Pilates Center offers a comprehensive program consisting of training on proper form, the purpose of each exercise, how to assess and adjust class members' posture and form, and how to properly pace the class to create an effective and comprehensive class. A certificate is awarded to those who complete 900 hours of formal lecture and internship work and pass several written and practical tests.

It is important to note that there are no nationally recognized standards for either yoga or pilates instruction. "Certified" training can be as short as a weekend course or as long as a multi-year program that is the equivalent of a college degree. According to the American Yoga Association, because yoga was historically passed down from teacher to student on an individual basis (creating many varieties and methods), it is unlikely that a standard training program for instruction will be created. Be sure to investigate your yoga or pilates training program to ensure that it is a quality program, and one suited to your own approach.

Other Requirements

Yoga and pilates instructors are expected to be flexible and physically fit, but they do not have to be in superhuman shape. Though the American Yoga Association has established a list of strict qualities that instructors should adhere to (maintain a vegetarian diet, act ethically), the basic qualities of every good instructor are the same: to be knowledgeable and passionate about your craft and be a patient and thorough instructor.

EXPLORING

The best way to explore these careers is to experience a yoga or Pilates class firsthand. In fact, you should attend several classes to learn the basics of the practice and build your skills. Ask to talk to the instructor after class about his or her job and how to get started. The instructor may recommend a certification program or give you names of other professionals to talk to about the practice.

You may also want to see if a local gym or community center has part-time positions available. Even if you are just working at the front desk, you will be able to see if you enjoy working in a health facility.

EMPLOYERS

Yoga and Pilates instructors work in fitness centers, gymnasiums, spas, dance studios, and community centers. Most employers are for-profit businesses, but some are community-based, such as the YMCA or a family center. Other job possibilities can be found in corporate fitness centers, colleges, nursing homes, hospitals, and resorts. In smaller towns, positions can be found in health care facilities, schools, and community centers.

STARTING OUT

If you have been attending yoga or pilates classes regularly, ask your instructor for ideas on training programs and if he or she knows of any job leads.

Often, facilities that provide training or internships will hire or provide job assistance to individuals who have completed programs. Students can also find jobs through classified ads and by applying to health and fitness clubs, YMCAs, YWCAs, community centers, local schools, park districts, religious groups, and other fitness organizations. Many companies now provide fitness facilities to their employees. As a result, students should consider nearby companies for prospective instructor positions.

ADVANCEMENT

Yoga and pilates instructors who have taught for several years and have the proper training can move into an instructor trainer position or, if they have the necessary capital, they may choose to establish their own private studio. To own a yoga or pilates studio, the instructor should be confident in his or her ability to attract new clients or be willing to ask old clients to move from their old class location to the new studio. With a bachelor's degree in either sports physiology or exercise physiology, instructors can advance to the position of health club director or to teach corporate wellness programs.

EARNINGS

According to the Pilates Method Alliance, pilates instructors usually charge $10 to $30 for group classes and $50 to $100 for an hour of personal instruction. CareerBuilder.com reports that yoga instructors who teach in community college extension programs earn an average of $35 per hour. Those who teach in private studios can earn from $30 to $40 per class, with some facilities paying more based on the number of students attending the class. Those who teach in corporate settings can earn $75 an hour or more. CareerBuilder.com reports that, in Los Angeles, successful yoga instructors can earn approximately $50,000 per year. Some highest-profile teachers earn more than $150,000 a year by charging their clients up to $250 an hour!

A compensation survey by health and fitness organization IDEA reports that many employers offer health insurance and paid sick and vacation time to full-time employees. They also may provide discounts on products sold in the club (such as shoes, clothing, and equipment) and free memberships to use the facility.

WORK ENVIRONMENT

Yoga and pilates classes are generally held indoors, in a studio or quiet room, preferably with a wooden floor. Classes can get crowded and hectic at times. Instructors need to keep a level head and maintain a positive personality in order to motivate class participants. They need to lead challenging, yet enjoyable, classes so that members return for more instruction.

OUTLOOK

Health professionals have long recommended daily aerobic exercise and resistance training to maintain weight, build strength, and improve overall health. But more recently, health professionals have added another recommendation: work on flexibility, posture, and stress reduction. These new concerns have given yoga and pilates a boost in popularity.

The U.S. Department of Labor predicts that the job outlook for fitness instructors should remain very strong over the next several years. As the average age of the population increases, yoga and Pilates instructors will find more opportunities to work with the elderly in retirement homes and assisted-living communities. Large companies and corporations, after realizing the stress reduction benefits of these "softer" forms of exercise, also hire yoga and pilates instructors to hold classes for their employees.

FOR MORE INFORMATION

For information on home study and various fitness certifications, contact
    American Fitness Professionals and Associates
    PO Box 214
    Ship Bottom, NJ 08008-0234
    Tel: 609-978-7583
    Email: afpa@afpafitness.com
    http://www.afpafitness.com

For more information about the practice, teaching, and origin of yoga, contact the following organizations:
    American Yoga Association
    PO Box 19986
    Sarasota, FL 34276-2986
    Tel: 941-927-4977
    http://www.americanyogaassociation.org

    Integral Yoga Teachers Association
    Route 1, Box 1720
    Buckingham, VA 23921
    Tel: 434-969-3121, ext. 137

Email: iyta@iyta.org
http://www.iyta.org

For fitness facts and articles, visit IDEA's Web site.
IDEA Health and Fitness Association
10455 Pacific Center Court
San Diego, CA 92121-4339
Tel: 800-999-4332
Email: contact@ideafit.com
http://www.ideafit.com

For training and certification information, contact
The Pilates Center
4800 Baseline Road, Suite D206
Boulder, CO 80303-2699
Tel: 303-494-3400
Email: info@thepilatescenter.com
http://www.thepilatescenter.com

For information about learning to practice and teach pilates, contact
Pilates Method Alliance
PO Box 370906
Miami, FL 33137-0906
Tel: 866-573-4945
Email: info@pilatesmethodalliance.org
http://www.pilatesmethodalliance.org

For information on registration for yoga teachers, contact
Yoga Alliance
7801 Old Branch Avenue, Suite 400
Clinton, MD 20735-1644
Tel: 877-964-2255
Email: info@yogaalliance.org
http://www.yogaalliance.org

INTERVIEW

Heather Barrett is a pilates instructor in Illinois. She teaches pilates in individual and class settings. Heather discussed her career with the editors of Careers in Focus: Coaches and Fitness Professionals.

Q. What made you want to become a pilates instructor?
A. I have been very involved in my own fitness for as long as I can remember. I played sports in high school—basketball, volleyball,

and softball. I also got into pilates because of a back problem I had about 10 years ago. I started doing pilates, and my back really got better. This is because of the strength I developed in my powerhouse (or core muscles). I started working as a pilates instructor because I thought it would be fun, and I want people to know how great pilates is for your body.

Q. What can high school students who are interested in this career do to learn more about the field?

A. High school students who are interested in this career should take a pilates class or take a private session and see if it is something they would like as an exercise format before they consider teaching it.

Q. What are the pros and cons of your job?

A. The pros of the job are being in shape and getting the opportunity to work with interesting people. The downside to this career is that the pay is not very good unless you open your own studio.

Q. What advice would you give to young people who are interested in becoming pilates instructors?

A. Follow what is in your heart. If you really want to become a pilates instructor, go for it, even if it doesn't pay a lot of money. Working just to make money in a job you don't like will be no fun, and you will always be looking for something better.

Index

Entries and page numbers in **bold** indicate major treatment of a topic.

A